Am
I
doing
this
right?

A philosophical guide to life
in the age of overwhelm

By Colleen Bordeaux

Am I doing this right?

By Colleen Bordeaux

Published by:
Colleen Bordeaux
Chicago, 60647 IL, USA

Typesetting: Donald Ruppert

Cover Design: Kostis Pavlou

A CIP record for this book is available from the Library of Congress Cataloging-in-Publication Data

ISBN-13: 978-0-578-52781-9

To my parents, for teaching me discipline, for valuing creativity, original thinking, and nurturing my inner writer from an extremely young age.

To my husband, for supporting and encouraging me to write this book, and for putting up with all of the long nights, early mornings, & mood swings that came with the process.

To everyone in the exquisitely uncool position of trying, failing, learning and growing, I see you, I am you, we'll be cool when we're dead, stay warm & keep going.

Contents

Introduction

"It's never too late to be who you might have been." - George Eliot

Not to be a Debbie Downer or anything, but we are all going to die. Hopefully not soon, but eventually and inevitably. Whatever it is inside of us that makes us who we are will cease to exist, and our bodies will rot. All that will remain of us will be the enduring elements of what we've focused on during our time on Earth, be it a building we've designed, a child we've raised, a book we've written—or something else entirely.

Did you know that there is danger in "mis-living" your life? In waking up one day and realizing you've totally wasted your one shot, that your life didn't matter or leave a mark in the way that it was supposed to?

That was a rhetorical question. Of course you know. You're reading a book titled, 'Am I doing this right?' So let's get on with it, shall we?

Most people mis-live their lives because they aren't clear on what they value or what really matters. They ask themselves the wrong questions (or no questions at all) about the most important areas of their lives, which leads to wrong answers, negative outcomes, and a lot of regret. They pursue goals that aren't worth attaining. They value stuff that doesn't matter, such as materialistic things or other people's opinions. They mold themselves to fit into the very narrow definition of success that our society touts. They spend time with life-sucking people who sap their joy. They can't figure out what will make them happy, so they eat, drink or shop their way into poor health, addiction, or not as much wealth as they'd like. Worst of all, they squish themselves into small, unnoticeable spaces carved out for them by their own fears and let life pass them by in a slow burn of mediocrity.

"The world offers you comfort. But you were not made for comfort. You were made for greatness." - Pope Benedict XVI

And then there are the rare people who die young at a very old age, who have lived incredibly fulfilling lives and leave in their wakes dozens, hundreds, thousands, even millions of people who were better off because they walked this Earth. They leave a ripple of infectious light, goodness and inspiration wherever they go, warming the hearts of people everywhere and coaxing those sad, squished people out of their cramped spaces, so they can live the lives they're truly capable of living.

You know these people. Every once in a while, you stumble across one of them when you least expect to, someone very brave who chose to strive for what you thought was not possible. Maybe you think that they're lucky, born with some advantage that the rest of us lack. But the reality is that they believed in possibilities for their life that you long ago shed as unrealistic for your own. They imagined for themselves a vision or an uncharted course, and summoned the courage to test the waters of their own capacities in a way that any so-called right-minded person would deem too risky, not fail-safe enough. And you look at them amazed, enchanted, offended, representing what you could have done in those pivotal moments of your life when you teetered between the practical and uncertain paths in front of you.

"If you ever find yourself in the wrong story, leave." - Mo Willems

Some of their names are emblazoned in books, on buildings, or in your memory. Others have lived lives of quiet brilliance, laying foundations of goodness for generations of family to come. They light a fire in those whose paths they cross, and unconsciously attract respect, wealth and every other resource the Universe has to offer in order to extend themselves in service to the world in their own way.

"If you plan on being anything less than you are capable of being, you will probably be unhappy all the days of your life." - Abraham Maslow

So why is it that so many of us croak at eighty, diseased and regretful of the lives we lived? Bronnie Ware, an Australian hospice nurse, observed her dying patients over many years and noticed some common themes that she published in her book "The Top 5 Regrets of the Dying." You know what their single biggest regret was? "I wish I had the courage to live a life true to myself, not the life others expected of me."

That is so effed up.

Let me say that a different way: there is nothing more tragic or depressing to me than knowing so many beautiful, wonderful, filled-with-potential human beings die this way. I don't want that for myself, or my family, or my friends, or my future children, or for you. So I wrote this book, after spending years obsessing over questions about how to realize my own life's potential.

They say that successful people ask better questions and, as a result, get better answers. My entire purpose for writing this book is I fundamentally believe that to be true, regardless of how you define success. Whether it's a fruitful career, a happy marriage, a vibrant child, or whatever your definition may be—the difference between you and someone who has what you imagine for yourself centers on the questions they've been willing to ask themselves and the answers they've had the courage to believe just enough to change their thinking.

"Your goal should be to waste as little of your life as possible." - John C. Maxwell

This book is a summary of the most important questions we need to ask ourselves in order to live our best lives. It's also a guide for how to answer those questions for yourself, drawing on input and wisdom from literally thousands of years of human thinking on those very questions, through the lenses of physicists, philosophers, psychologists, theologians, and a whole host of other frameworks our species has used to understand these important topics.

This is going to sound grandiose (because it is), but I believe this will be the most important book you ever read. I am 100 percent biased because I wrote it, but I will give you your money back in 80 years if you read the content in this very short book, put it into practice in your own life, and end up staring death in the face talking about your regrets to someone like Bronnie Ware.

It's because I am confident that the knowledge in these pages will help you to become an ancient, crispy, vivacious old human laughing at your own jokes and relishing in the joy of the past century or so that you've lived. And you'll be doing this while biking through Tuscan vineyards, double-fisting glasses of the most expensive red wine ever made surrounded by people you love.

If you're thinking, "Colleen, what if I don't want to be a drunk 105-year-old on a unicycle?" I hear you. Just insert whatever image of living your most joyful life up to the last drop means to you, and know that this book intends to help you create that vision for real. Because we all have a limited attention span and you may now have a burning desire to figure out whether or not you've been asking yourself the right questions, I'll just go ahead and cut to the chase.

Why I'm qualified to write this book:

After spending far too much time caring about things that didn't matter, I had a full-fledged quarter-life crisis. I was para- lyzed with indecision, signing apartment leases, then canceling the check, interviewing and accepting jobs, then reneging, waffling on what city to live in, plagued with FOMO ('fear of missing out', for anyone lucky enough to be unfamiliar with that terrible affliction), and insecure from comparing myself to other people. In fact, I *almost* broke up with my now-husband because I thought he liked me too much and how could that be possible if I was such a hot mess? In a nutshell, I was not chill about anything, overanalyzed everything and generally sucked at life.

The reality was, I'd never asked myself a critical question, period. I knew I wanted a fulfilling career and a happy life, a wonderful relationship and a healthy body, but I'd never really considered how to define those things according to my own standards and cut through the noise of our world to figure out how to bring those goals to life for myself.

This little meltdown phase led me down a self-development wormhole that's lasted for more than seven years, facilitated by a career in management consulting where I've spent an average of 80 percent of my time traveling with hours of flight time to read each week. According to my calculations, I've spent 190,460 hours reading 3,640 books on the topic of human potential, covering philosophy, theology, psychology, and other related genres, spanning roughly 2,500 years of human thinking from ancient Greek philosophers to modern-day Tony Robbins.

Call me obsessed, a self-help savant, or avoiding my under-developed identity with books, but you'll be hard-pressed to find someone with more ideas under her belt on the subject. Okay, maybe Oprah. And I've had results (*high fives self*), solely attributed to what I've learned and applied from these books: I started listening to the inner voice in my head and stopped listening to almost everything else, married the love of my life, created the career of my dreams working alongside Harvard MBAs with a measly print-editorial journalism degree, quadrupled my income in a few short years, and got into the best physical shape of my life while sitting at a desk for fourteen hours a day. It's all the books, I tell you! Powerful stuff in there!

I wrote this book not as an expert on anything, but as a normal person with real problems who learned and tested life-changing ideas and solutions from many amazing thinkers who were nice enough to document their brilliance for the rest of us. This book is a simple attempt to pay it forward to those who can benefit from what I've learned, but don't have a spare 190,460 hours or interest in reading 3,640 self-help books. Consider it your self-development starter set and reading list on steroids, organized around the foundational questions we should be asking ourselves about the most important areas of our lives, with recommendations on further reading based on the best books I've discovered along the way.

I sincerely hope you find it valuable. If you don't, I look for-ward to chatting in year 2099.

Before we go any further, a disclaimer for my haters:

Some people might think that writing a whole book about life philosophy is dumb, calling out my privilege and noting how frivolous it is to talk about things like potential and confidence when we have so much more to solve for. Wars! Starvation! Unequal distribution of access to resources! Micro-aggression! Actual aggression! Depression! Global warming! Children dying at the border! Noise pollution! Mental illness! Mass shootings! You get the idea.

There are a lot of people much smarter than me who are thinking and talking about the most critical issues of our world, which is important. My point-of-view is that, ultimately, these problems need more than thinking and talking.

Although it might be easier to simply read about the world's problems in The New Yorker from your first class plane seat, sipping a glass of free mediocre chardonnay, feeling distressed yet powerless to change anything given the narrow parameters you've built around your life, it doesn't actually solve anything.

Our world needs solutions, which tend to come from people who believe in themselves enough to actually do something, paying forward their privileges and gifts for the benefit of the world.

That's what fulfilling your life's potential looks like, and there aren't enough people in this world who do that. I wrote this book because I believe the reason people live far beneath their potential is because they haven't been asking themselves the right questions, and our world suffers as a result.

So here we are.

End of disclaimer.

Ok, where were we? Ah yes, the only 7 questions that matter in life. I've conveniently organized each question into a chapter for you:

Chapter 1: Who the eff am I? An introduction to self and identity

Chapter 2: Why am I running around in this meat suit? An overview of purpose and vocation

Chapter 3: Speaking of my meat suit, is there a user guide? A foundation for keeping your body healthy as long as you care to live

Chapter 4: What about that big blob of cholesterol that tells me what to do? An orientation to mind control

Chapter 5: Who the eff are these people? A fundamental truth about the power of the company you keep

Chapter 6: How do I pay for this? An attitude on acquiring wealth

Chapter 7: Where am I meant to end up? A beginner's perspective on how to let go of your white-knuckle grip on life

This book is intended to be a living document that you can revisit again and again, a tool that you can use to structure your thinking and help you identify the right questions to ask yourself in order to gain clarity and confidence in the most important aspects of your life. In the following pages, we'll explore seven major questions and work through exercises to help you answer them for yourself.

These questions, in my experience, are sequential, building an increasingly stronger foundation for developing your life after you've considered and answered them for yourself. So if you've already got a few of them covered, feel free to skip ahead. Or read them for pure entertainment value, because I spent an inordinate amount of time on the jokes.

Ok, let's go.

CHAPTER 1

Who the eff am I?

An introduction to self & identity

Other forms of this question include everything you've ever thought to yourself about yourself.

"You lack nothing, use what I gave you." - God

The reason this is the first *real* chapter of this short book is because how you feel about who you are—how that inner voice in your head talks to you about who you are—is the most important factor in determining whether you live a long and fulfilling life, or die with regrets. How you feel about yourself manifests itself into every single aspect of your life, determining the quality of your relationships, your health, and the success you enjoy (or not). Your sense of self has nothing to do with your parents, or your opportunities (or lack thereof), or your looks, or your talents. It has everything to do with the experiences you have inside of your own mind.

Each of us was born with a perfect, innate sense of self who knew that we were welcome in the world, that we were valuable, worthy and enough exactly as we were, simply because we existed. We inherently knew the Universe would provide for us, crying out when we were hungry with absolute expectation that our needs would be met. We rested in this inherently worthy sense of self as a baby, and it's why we were so happy and ate birthday cake with such messy gusto and wanted nothing more than to be with the people who made us laugh. As babies, our minds hadn't been trained to synthesize all of the external inputs required to start judging, doubting, fearing and all of the other negative thought patterns that drown out the voice of this worthy, innate sense of self that knows it is enough simply because it exists.

For the first couple years of our lives, the rest of the world agrees that we're inherently enough exactly as we are, treating us as these tiny blobs of limitless potential, holding all hope of advancing the human species in the grasp of our chubby, sticky hands. Just observe a new mom for a few minutes and you'll see what I'm talking about. Or, imagine trying to rationalize with a baby that it is not enough: "Listen, baby. You're chubby, you're bald, you literally know nothing, you poop in your own pants and rely on the kindness of others to live to see tomorrow. Look at all those cute, little preemies in the cribs around you. Compared to those tiny dolls, you and your jaundice and your ten pound birth weight make you look like a pumpkin. No one will ever love you."

It's so ridiculous! No one would talk to a baby like that! But somewhere between day one of life and wherever we are now, we learn to believe and say those kinds of things to ourselves. So why is that? Why do so many of us spend mental energy thinking that we're not enough, comparing ourselves to others, and convincing ourselves that we're coming up lacking? We conflate our value with our jobs, our appearance, our belongings, and how other people see us.

It's because we grow up slowly collecting a layer of beliefs and expectations from our families and cultures, and we unconsciously roll them into our sense of who we are. At some point, our perfect, innately worthy self we were born with starts noticing the ways that it is different, and begins to internalize that it is not enough. We eat Play Doh because we know it's delicious and benign, but everyone at daycare tells us we're disgusting so we start to believe them. We suck at hopscotch and get shamed on the playground, so we stop playing and watch sadly from the sidelines. We eventually have so many of these experiences where our limitless joy in exploring who we are in relationship to the world is met with resistance and negativity from others, that we forget all about the perfect, innately worthy self within us.

Instead of resting in the confidence that we're worthy and enough exactly as we are, we allow this residue of other people's beliefs and expectations cloud who we really are and what we truly care about. We start to think that we are not worthy, capable, or enough and learn to look for external validation in how we think, act and carry ourselves. It leads us to lack a coherent sense of who we are and uncertainty about what we want to do with our lives. It's the root cause of an unfulfilling life, and the reason why most people "lead lives of quiet desperation" according to Thoreau.

Most people don't even realize that they're spending their precious days on Earth ignoring their innately worthy self and living according to everyone else's standards but their own. They never stop to ask themselves who they really are or what they really value. It's why so many people have identity crises during big upheavals or major milestones in life, because those moments require us to fall back on our core, innately worthy self for strength. If we haven't taken the time to peel back the layers of other people's expectations to really get to know and rest in our true selves buried within us, those moments can be the most painful and destructive pivot points in our lives.

"We have to really educate ourselves in a way about who we are, what our real identity is." - Deepak Chopra

If you're slightly worried that you've been living a quiet, desperate life and suffocating your innately worthy self, it's cool. So many people are in the same situation. I totally was. We can fix this! And it will be exciting, because "who am I, and who do I want to be?" is one of the most amazing and terrifying questions we can ask ourselves.

And to answer this question, we need to understand what we really mean when we say "true self," because that sounds nebulous ay-eff. On that note, let's start with a quick aside on the concepts of identity and "true self":

Walt Whitman once wrote that "we contain multitudes," referring to how we see ourselves as radically different depending on context. For example, I routinely present my expertise to client executives at work, but just last week I crumbled when I tried to explain the purpose of this book to my elementary school gym teacher aunt. In a corporate setting, I'm a confident, assertive leader who is clear on the value that I bring to the table. In a passive-aggressive Midwest family party context, I revert to the fifteen-year-old version of myself with a bad haircut, braces, glasses, and an underdeveloped sense of who I am and what I am qualified to speak about.

Pioneering identity researcher Erik Erikson suggested that each of us develop a continuous and enduring sense of self by combining all the different versions of who we are into an "ego identity" that creates our core identity. We define ourselves around different roles (e.g., daughter, sister, wife, mom, friend, consultant, etc.), as well as positive and negative attributes (e.g., Catholic, disorganized, intelligent, imposter, attractive, etc.), and this enduring sense of self—your beliefs about who you are—essentially drives your thoughts, decisions, behaviors, and life outcomes.

"Every person is composed of a few themes." - C.S. Lewis

Most people don't realize that they have a choice in continuing to behave according to their ego identity, and that they have the ability to craft an identity true to who they really are. Basically, I'm saying the whole cliche that "you can be anything you wanna be" is true after all, but the cliche left out the instructions (dang those cliches, they always do).

You have to ask yourself questions that make you go inside of yourself for answers. The people who put the thought, energy, and courage into getting back in touch with their innately worthy self, and intentionally decide who they want to be are the ones who live incredibly fulfilling lives that leave wakes behind them when they exit this planet.

Before I get into the weeds on how to start getting back in touch with your innately worthy self and intentionally deciding who you want to be, I'd like to share a brief personal anecdote about my own identity crisis that led me down a wormhole of reading and research on this exact topic and helped me to answer it for myself.

My personal struggle with this question:

"To be nobody but yourself, in a world which does its best, day and night, to make you like everyone else, means to fight the hardest battle any human being can ever fight and never stop fighting" - E.E. Cummings

The first time I read the above quote, I was in eighth grade. It was the end of the school year, and my language arts teacher gave it to me on a printed sheet of green stationary with a lady-bug border. She must have sensed that I needed the inspiration, judging by my bowl cut, glasses, braces, violin case, and toolbox filled with art supplies that I carried to school every day for my extra-curricular activities.

I spent Friday nights making structures out of balsa wood and then crushing them with my Odyssey of the Mind team. (For those not up to speed on terminology of American nerds, "Odyssey of the Mind" is a creative problem-solving program where students work on a pre-defined problem and present their solutions in competitions. For some reason, every competition involves creating a structure out of balsa wood to be crushed with giant bodybuilder weights. IDK why I did this, probably because it was the only club that would accept me).

My favorite outfit was a purple corduroy jumper paired with an olive green turtleneck, accentuated by my knobby knees and size ten Doc Marten Mary Janes, which I topped with a gray North Face fleece jacket that I'd paid for, in cash, with babysitting money in order to have the socially acceptable outerwear of my peer group. My parents drove me and my five siblings around town in a giant red Ford Club Wagon van that we dubbed "The Church Bus" for both its cavernous capacity and lack of street credibility. It instilled in me a deep love of walking and public transportation.

It would have been so much easier to have just been cool. To have had the right looks, the right talents, the right hobbies, the right friends, the right clothes, etc. I'd tried (and failed at) all of the things that makes one cool in middle school, including preparing a solo acapella audition—with dance moves, might I add, because I was truly committed—for Show Choir where I was cut for lacking the talent to back up my stage presence. It was a series of crushing defeats that helped me to realize that I wasn't going to be beautiful or popular, so I might as well be smart and develop a good personality.

Mark Twain once said that the worst loneliness is to not be comfortable with yourself. And it's a concept that I know well from various stages of my life, including the most pronounced as a twelve-year-old testing the waters of my own innate abilities (like filming Richard Simmons-esque turn-of-the-century workout videos complete with hoop skirts and butter-churning cardio moves) and inabilities (like all things involving hand-eye coordination) and considering where my strengths fit in a world where writing haikus and taking watercolor classes with middle-aged women did not exactly lead to conventionally successful outcomes.

I remember feeling out of place and unsure of myself often as a girl, reinforced by experiences where I thought I had it all together, and then learned that, in fact, I did not. For example, that time I showed up to gym class in FUBU socks that I bought at TJ Maxx assuming they were like Reebok, thinking they looked sharp with my uniform. I was dismayed to learn that they were not anything like Reebok, but, instead, a tough urban menswear brand that looked ridiculous on my bony ankles attached to my ninety pound body. On me, those FUBU socks had the opposite effect for a brand that claims to make clothes "…for people who do not want to stand out but want to be seen."

Sorry, where were we? Ah yes, that E.E. Cummings quote that my middle school teacher gave to me, not realizing that it was going to be a lifelong gift of inspiration to be true to myself, no matter how hard that can sometimes be in a reality when you're wearing FUBU socks and getting shamed by a group of middle school boys.

We spend most of our lives accumulating the expectations of other people: our parents, our siblings, our friends, our teachers, our culture, our social circles, our communities, and so on. Some of those expectations are good in that they encourage us to develop good character. Most of those expectations are entirely bogus and have the power to make us doubt ourselves, feel less than, or not loveable or worthy enough. And they're exactly the kinds of beliefs we need to peel back in order to rest in our innately worthy selves and live up to the potential we were born with. Here are a few personal examples of the kinds of bogus expectations that I'm talking about:

When I moved to a new city after college, a friend of my cousin's called me ugly and not that great, definitely not good enough to join her clique. Although I pretended it didn't matter at the time, it cut deeply and made me overanalyze my appearance and doubt myself, my worth, and my lovability. At one point, I actually worried that one side of my jaw was slightly lower than the other and considered getting a nose job to solve for that big ol' thing of cartilage in the center of my face gifted to me by my northern European forebears.

When I first started working in management consulting, a manager with several Ivy League degrees told me that my mediocre state university in the Midwest wasn't good enough and would get me nowhere, advising that I do everything in my power to get into an elite graduate school and deemphasize my background. Although I laughed it off as a joke, it made me question my intelligence, my value, and my future. Even though everything in my soul was calling me to create, to get off the corporate treadmill, I bought a GMAT book and started the process of studying and applying to get the pedigree that I was lacking, rationalizing away my fears about taking on hundreds of thousands of dollars of debt that would tie me to a career path that didn't feel quite right.

When I got engaged, some family members told me that it was unlikely that my marriage would survive because my fiancé was not Catholic, that we'd struggle without the security of common values, beliefs, and familial cultural norms neatly tied together under the banner of religion. Despite being deeply in love with my fiancé, it made me question my priorities when it came to choosing a life partner and doubt my abilities to make such a life-changing decision, and I would stress every time we had a disagreement because of it.

When I started blogging and freelance writing, a few colleagues told me it was dumb, would limit my potential, and I should quit or keep it really quiet. Even though writing brought me so much joy, it made me deeply ashamed of what I was producing. I remember walking through O'Hare on my way to a huge meeting with an important client and deciding that it was time to delete the blog and hunker down on my practical path, afraid that a client would Google me, find my half-baked creativity on full display and fire me. So, I pretended like my creative work didn't matter and kept it in a small, safe place, allowing myself to believe that other people's opinions were more important than my own.

We all have experiences like these. For me, these experiences helped me to find my true self and listen to my inner voice, because although I struggled with the expectations and judgments of other people, accepting them as my own was not an option. There was no way I was going to absorb the belief that I was ugly and unlovable, or that I needed to pay hundreds of thousands of dollars for a degree to succeed, or that I should dump my fiancé to find someone who could check the box on the "right religious background," or that I should step back from my love of writing. Looking back, I realize that each of the people in those examples were struggling with insecurity and fear, and probably trying to stay safe in whatever warped way they defined it.

These glaring experiences also helped highlight some of the smaller, seemingly innocuous ways that I'd been allowing other people's expectations drive my behavior, especially in how I spent my time and money. It was really bad, but the good news is that I fixed it! I found my true self, the delightful human being writing to you from the other side of this book! And I am going to tell you how I did it, and share the exact steps I went from doubting myself, my abilities and pretty much everything that I was doing, to knowing and trusting my true self and using it as a guiding light and source of confidence in my life.

The process involved years of reading and reflection, but it didn't need to. The steps were actually quite simple, and I've included the best ideas from the accumulated wisdom of the world that helped me complete them.

"You change the world by being yourself." - Yoko Ono

How to answer this question for yourself:

If you haven't figured it out by now, the short answer to the question of, "Who the eff am I?" is that you're still the inherently worthy, perfect little baby-self you were born as, and beyond that, you are whoever the eff you want to be. It doesn't matter where you're from or who your family is or what you look like or how much money you make or what your job is. None of that defines you.

The process of finding your true self rests on taking back the clean slate of your future. You can go back to that little baby self who never doubts for one second her worth, or whether she's enough, or how her basic needs will be met. She understands that she is valuable, that she is welcome in the world, that she has nothing to fear, and that anything she wants is hers for the taking.

In case you (or one of my siblings) is thinking that I'm suggesting that you're supposed to just forget your past, that's not the case. Instead, it's channeling those experiences as a source of strength to change how you think going forward, a reason to trust in everything that you are, regardless of what anyone else might think, and drown out the fears that prevent you from staying true to yourself.

"Ever loved someone so much that you would do anything for them? Yeah, well, make that someone yourself and do whatever the hell you want." - Harvey Specter

That perfect baby self is still in you, waiting for you to rest in the truth that you are worthy and enough exactly as you are, and simply build from there. You have the choice, today, to leave behind whoever you've been in the past, whatever mistakes you've made or trials you've overcome or circumstances you've inherited. You have the choice to consciously let go of all of the residue you've built up over the course of your life that has led you to doubt yourself, your worth and your value to the world.

You can literally change the entire course of who you are becoming in an instant, isn't that a relief? The only thing that defines who you are and who you will be in the future is what you think and decide and do in this exact moment—and every moment to follow.

As you might imagine, the hard part about getting back to your innately worthy self who believes she is enough exactly as she is, and then building yourself into whoever the eff you want to be, is actually doing it.

"I needed to be myself and find my own identity." - Bill Skarsgard

One of the most mind-blowing ideas on how to do this came from a very old book written in the 1930s by a guy named Charles Haanel called "The Master Key System" (a book that my husband believes brainwashed me—he freaks out every time I bring it up, which is usually once per day since I first read it five years ago). Anyway, in this book, Haanel argues that your ability to think about your own thoughts suggests that there are two "selves" in you: your conscious, thinking mind, as well as a 'spiritual self' that is an entity beyond your mind, sitting above it with the ability to direct it.

Haanel didn't use these words, but this other "self" is the innately worthy one we've been talking about this whole chapter, the one you rested in as a baby, never doubting your inherent value and potential. That self is still present in you, available for you to channel, experience and enjoy every bit of yourself, regardless of any person, belief, event or other external thing that's been clouding it since you last relished in it as a baby.

What a beautiful concept, this idea of "resting in" your inherently valuable self that is worthy simply by being, regardless of your circumstances, appearance, effed up family or failures. I believe, in my core, that each of our 'spiritual' or higher selves, are connected to a larger truth that thousands of years of human thinking has yet to define and truly understand.

Our connection to something that is beyond human (regardless of what we may call it—intelligent design, God, the Universe, nothing or something else entirely) is the foundation of our inherent value. Even if you don't believe this, if you've read this far into the chapter, you have absolutely nothing to lose by humoring the idea that your existence is connected to something beyond what we can possibly understand, and use it as a source of confidence to overcome the human-created nonsense that limits your potential.

So without further ado, here are the steps to take help figure out who the eff you are:

#1 Find your higher self in your own mind.

Stop what you're doing, right now, and think about what is happening in your thoughts. Can you do it? What's swirling around in there? If you are able to think about your own thoughts, you've found your higher self. It amazes me every time I do this exercise, how easy it is to press pause on my racing mind and find that calm voice of my true self who wants me to simmer the eff down.

If you can't find that higher self because your mind won't stop racing, I get it. You're going to need to brainwash yourself by faking, for a while, that you have this little hype squad between your ears telling you how amazing you are at all times. Meditation helps, too. (I hesitate in writing that, because I am definitely someone who needs a book on meditation for Type A neurotics who cannot sit still. It would be called "Uncomfortably staring into space, with coffee.")

#2 Identify your negative self-talk.

This shouldn't be hard. It's all the nonsense you've been telling yourself for years, that you're not [insert adjective] enough, or you're not a good [insert noun], or you're ugly or a failure or whatever. It's also the thoughts that might be directed at others, judgmental thoughts driven by fear. Negative thinking about other people also falls into the negative self-talk category, because it clouds the positive, productive thinking you need to grow—you cannot afford to have thoughts in your head about yourself or any other person that conflict with your innately worthy self.

It's impossible to be confident and consistently effective in fulfilling your life purpose if you are not continually training your mind to align to the positive, productive, life-giving truth of your higher self.

So how do we do this? Imagine pressing pause on your self-talk and writing it in quotes. Write as many of them down as you can think of. Know that you can't stop negative self-talk from popping up—it's always lurking, waiting to be triggered, especially in moments when you're stressed, haven't slept or eaten, or when you try on a pair of jeans that just went through the wash, get a zit, or get criticized at work. The key is training yourself to identify and kill it before it takes hold, and make room for better thoughts.

#3 Sic your higher self on your negative self-talk.

This will be hard, because you're actively retraining your mind to eliminate unproductive external beliefs that have collected over time. It will take a lot of energy at first, but over time you will rewire your thoughts until it becomes effortless. Every single time you catch yourself in a negative thought loop, press pause in your mind and summon your higher self to take a look at those negative thoughts. Then use her to kill them. Use that space where the now-dead negative thought existed to ask yourself what better thought can you put in its place.

For me, when my anxious mind sets in, I summon my higher self to replace anxiety with gratitude: "Colleen, what do you even have to worry about?! Look at the abundance around you!" Call it summoning the power of the universe or tuning in to the Holy Spirit or simply brainwashing yourself, I don't care. If you put in the time and energy, it works. And it creates the most amazing and enduring sense of peace and a zero-effs-given kind of confidence that is 100 percent under your control and requires absolutely no change in external circumstances.

This takes work, but over time, becomes automatic. If you think it's crazy to stop all negative self-talk in its tracks by summoning your higher self, I guarantee you've never tried it. I challenge you to give yourself a twenty-four-hour period to test this theory. Start right now. Set an alarm on your phone for tomorrow at this exact time to check in, then climb right into your own head, camp out there and watch those crazy thoughts fly by. Summon your higher self to squash them as they pop up, like she's playing a game of Whack-a-mole. I don't care what the thought is or how much your lower self thinks it is based in facts. Just kill it, and put a positive, productive one in its place.

See how you feel in twenty-four hours. It's going to change everything. At a minimum, it will help you realize how many negative thoughts you are allowing to hold you back from being the best version of yourself. And letting negative thinking drive your life is so two-thousand-and-late, if you know what I mean.

Summary of the key takeaway from this chapter:

You are inherently valuable, worthy, and loved just for being born and existing. Your perfect little baby self is still under all those layers of nonsense begging for you to rest in the inner joy you were born with and be whoever the eff you want to be. It's time to start squashing the negative thinking, and resuscitate your inherently worthy self who's been there all along.

Recommended books with more research, ideas, and practical tips to answer this question:

The Ancient Stoic Art of Joy by William B. Irvine
Living Buddha, Living Christ by Thich Nhat Hanh
The Master Key System by Charles Haanel
In Search of Identity by Anwar el Sadat
Perfectly Yourself by Matthew Kelly
The Divine Dance by Richard Rohr

CHAPTER 2

Why am I running around in this meat suit?

An overview of life purpose

Other forms of this question include statements like, "I am a marketer of the eighth-most-popular brand of individually packaged potato chips and work in a tall building in the city. It is prudent and economically secure and does not make me profoundly unhappy. Sometimes I am able to leave in time to make it to Soul Cycle. No one loves their job all the time."

"This is the true joy in life, the being used for a purpose recognized by yourself as a mighty one; the being a force of nature instead of a feverish, selfish, little cloud of ailments and grievances complaining that the world will not devote itself to making you happy… I want to be thoroughly used up when I die, for the harder I work the more I live. I rejoice in life for its own sake. Life is no brief candle to me. It is a

sort of splendid torch which I have got hold of for the moment, and I want it to burn as brightly as possible before handing it on to future generations." - George Bernard Shaw

If you've ever had the feeling that what you're doing isn't quite in line with what you're supposed to be doing, you are far from alone. We're all here on Earth running around in these meat suits wondering what the eff to do with ourselves. (Ok, we all know 'dress the meat suit'… but I feel like that's been a given since Adam and Eve ate the apple in the Garden of Eden and ruined nudity for all of mankind.)

Anyway, where were we? Oh yes. Why we're here. It's the ultimate existential question, and we're living in a point in human history where we have a paradox of more time than ever to think about it, but a harder time than ever to answer it, according to Barry Schwartz, author of The Paradox of Choice. Schwartz pointed out that the greater number of choices we have, the harder it becomes to choose, and it leads to dissatisfaction and analysis paralysis.

A nihilist would argue that we're all here on Earth by random chance, that nothing matters, that we're all going to die and that there is no "why" to our existence. Some other philosophical camps would agree, and while guzzling wine and being fed tiny bites of cheese by forced laborers, add that because nothing matters, we should focus on maximizing our pleasure here on Earth. Not only is this idea that nothing matters utterly depressing (WTF, Nietzsche?!), but fundamentally untrue.

In her inspiring TED Talk titled "How to stop screwing yourself over," Mel Robbins talks about how a mathematician calculated that the odds of you being born, exactly as you are, is about 1 in 400 trillion. That number considered all sorts of chance happenings, like the tiny split-second decision your mom made when she decided to go to that party in the late 70s when she really felt like washing her hair and going to bed early, the synapses that fired in your dad's mind when he saw her and decided to mosey on over with the world's lamest pick up line—which worked, much to his surprise—and millions of other variables that led to your conception and birth versus someone else entirely. So meta, especially if you think backwards on all the "should-have-stayed-in-and-washed-my-hair" moments that led to the birth of your parents' parents!

My point is that you beat some odds to be here, and there's a reason you beat out all those trillions of potential souls to grace us all here on Earth with your presence. It's because you're here for a very specific reason, a reason that you are responsible for discovering and living out, and it does not involve getting fat n' sassy in front of a television regretting the circumstances of your life and wishing things could be different.

Also, there is a very important caveat that comes with the topic of life purpose that most people don't realize. And it's this: every single privilege you were born with, that so many of the other seven billion other people here on Earth were not, exponentially deepens your responsibility to find and use your purpose for the benefit of the world. For example, I am going to assume that if you are reading this book, you are literate and have at least $10 worth of disposable income which puts you way up on top of the world population when it comes to privilege.

It's your responsibility to use that privilege to make something of yourself, to be of value, to do something to ease the burden of others who didn't get to enjoy the same stroke of luck in this life. Barry Schwartz described our excess of choices as the ultimate first world problem, and until we solve for opportunity redistribution, we must use our privilege to increase our individual abilities to give back to the world.

The tough thing about purpose is that there's not a black-and-white answer, a specific career or entrepreneurial venture or particular path that wraps it up for you in a nice little bow. It's the whole of your existence, of how you become a net positive in the lives of the people whose paths you cross.

That last paragraph is extremely important. Your job does not translate into your purpose, and the false belief that you can "find a job you're passionate about" has led a lot of people to waste big chunks of their lives chasing some abstraction of life purpose that does not exist. My personal hero, Dr. Meg Jay, wrote a book about this false belief called 'The Defining Decade' that saved me from my early 20s identity crisis.

"Forget about having an identity crisis and get some identity capital. ... Do something that adds value to who you are. Do something that's an investment in who you might want to be next." - Dr. Meg Jay, brilliant psychologist, author of The Defining Decade

If you've ever said, "I don't know what my life purpose is so I'm just going to travel the world for a while until I figure it out," I have some very bad news for you: you'll never find it that way, and Dr. Meg Jay will layer on that this is a great strategy if you'd also like to be poor and miserable later in life.

So if you can't find your purpose on a one-way, around-the-world ticket, how are you supposed to find it? To find it, you need to know what you're looking for—and it's not a job or a career path or a simple answer.

The purpose of your life, and my life, and every single person's life on Earth is to add value to other people, period. Let me say that a different way: the purpose of your life has nothing to do with you, and everything to do with how your life helps to make someone else's better, simpler, or happier. According to pretty much every philosopher, economist, religious framework, and even capitalism. If you're focused on fame, money, glory or pleasure, you will die unhappy, guaranteed. The facts say so! The smartest scientist of the last century says so! "Only a life lived for others is a life worthwhile," according to Albert Einstein himself.

You might think that living a life for others requires a lot of sacrifice, patience and other holier-than-thou skills that you may or may not have. Let me be the first one to tell you that this is not true. (If you were to ask any of my siblings if I have those skills, I guarantee they would die of laughter.) My point is, serving others in the way that you're here to do will energize and expand your capacity to do what you're meant to be doing.

We are meant to exude joy in what we do every day. It's the most amazing power we have, to spread love, positivity and goodness through our very presence. When you think about that fact, it's not surprising that people seek pleasure, happiness and instant gratification. When we feel bad, we want to return to feeling good as quickly as possible and grab at the things that seem the easiest, like food, approval, money or whatever. The paradox is that the pursuit of those things has the exact opposite effect. It might provide some temporary reprieve, but doesn't resolve the hole.

If what you're doing exhausts you, you're not living your purpose, because you are not exuding joy, energy, enthusiasm and spreading light to other people who desperately need it. Instead, you're taking the place of someone else who should be doing that work in a way that makes a far greater impact on lives than you ever will in that space. Meanwhile, all of the people your life is supposed to touch aren't benefiting one bit from you walking around in your meat suit emanating bad vibes. They're sad, they need your joy, act now! To put this in Marie Kondo terms (which is how we will all communicate by the time this book is published), give the stuff you do a hug, thank the stuff, and then throw it into a Goodwill box because it's not sparking anything and you need to clear out your life for what does.

So what is the source of joy, and how do we produce more of it in our lives? The answer is that joy comes from giving of our best selves to others, and by far the greatest thing you have to give other people is your love, enthusiasm, excitement, passion, and energy. Giving those things in a way that is authentic to who you really are gives you power to share and spread your light. And when you do that, you unconsciously give others permission to do the same.

"Work is love made visible. And if you cannot work with love but only with distaste, it is better that you should leave your work and sit at the gate of the temple and take aims of those who work with joy." - Khalil Gibran

It's like dominos for positivity! I trademarked that last sentence so don't even try to steal it. Let me say that a different way: the purpose of your life is to find those things that light you up and to create space in your life to do more of them. Maybe what lights you up is creating restrictive panty hose that makes other women feel confident in their own butts. Or maybe you really love competitive fencing that makes other people feel like they should come out into the open with their secret love of lost medieval sports. Whatever lights you up is where you're supposed to be focusing the energy and time you've been given in this life, period. As Joseph Campbell said, "Follow your bliss."

You might be thinking that you're not sure what you have to offer that lights you up and adds value to other people. And the reality is that there's no simple way to answer this question, as much as we love to think getting an Ivy League MBA or a new baby or a winning lottery ticket might answer it for us. You have to do a lot of work and do a lot of things that you don't like in order to figure out your unique talents and what lights you up, versus what saps your energy. The key is to work, experiment, learn, and pay attention so you can make strategic changes that create more space for activities that fulfill you.

You also have to figure out what problems you care about enough to solve. In his amazing book, Originals, Adam Grant shares proof that those who change the world for the better aren't unusually smart or especially talented — nor do they have unusual passion or even much of an appetite for risk. Instead, they simply saw a problem that no one else was addressing, and took a different approach to solving it.

Simply put, anyone can think differently, take action, and improve the world in their own way.

Knowing your passions and identifying the right arenas in which to use them to add value to other people rests in our ability to put in the time to truly understand ourselves in more concrete detail, to define what problems we care to solve, to pinpoint what lights us up versus what saps our joy, and pro-actively orient the balance in our favor.

You may be expecting me to give you some cliché and nebulous advice about how to do this, like "Meditate on it until you're struck with inspiration!" And that would be a great way to guarantee that you and every other person who bought this book will be hunting me down in eighty years to insist on your money back, ruining my drunk unicycle ride in Tuscany.

"There are two great days in a person's life: the day you're born, and the day you discovered why." - John C. Maxwell

Instead, I am going to give you a very concrete, practical exercise you can do, right now, to clarify what the eff you're here on Earth to do. This simple framework helped me bring into focus what I was uniquely positioned to do with my time and talents in this world. It's the reason I have a job that I love and have built a freelance writing hustle on the side, and why I wrote this book. But first, a story to set context around this exercise.

My personal struggle with this question:

When I started my first job in management consulting, I went in with soaring expectations and a shiny new collection of Brooks Brothers suits. I'd studied hard for my case interviews, researched the firm at length, and knew in my soul that it was "what I was meant to do," whatever that meant.

I utterly despised it within a week of my start date.

And by "utterly despised," I mean my body had a visceral reaction and everything in me was telling me to quit. Think sleepless nights, midday tears in the bathroom, and an unshakable urge to flee. (Isn't it strange how our bodies rebel when we hate something? No judgment if being a sleep-deprived lunatic is your thing.)

If I am being totally honest, it also gave me a confidence-shattering case of doubt in myself and my ability to make big decisions, such as choosing a career path. I couldn't put my finger on exactly what it was that drove such a deep emotional response in me, but I didn't want to suffer through the time required to reflect. I wanted out, ASAP. I remember standing at Starbucks waiting for my latte and envying the barista, because she seemed so content and focused on what she was doing for the packed room of people.

So, as an anxious 20-something does, I began frantically applying for jobs, spraying my resume all over the place with an earnest hope that the answer would simply land in my lap. There was an operational role for a retailer in Japan, an editorial job at a media company in NYC, and at least a million others that I considered. My only criteria was that it was not my current position.

One day after I accepted a role that would take me far from Washington, D.C., my friends and my relationship with my now-husband, I met a woman at my firm's office who sensed my distress (and by "sensed," I mean "accidentally walked into a conference room and found me sobbing") and gave me the best career advice I've ever received:

"Never run from, only to, a position," she said. "You need to figure out what you want, and then take logical steps to get it." She asked me to slow down and take time to complete a simple exercise in structuring my thoughts, and if I still wanted to make that decision afterwards, I should be confident moving forward.

Taking her advice helped me to make the right decisions to better align how I spent my time towards activities and problems I cared about, and I'm convinced that I would be in a dramatically different place today if I hadn't completed this honest assessment of myself. In fact, I saved my original notes and revisit them periodically to see if I need to refine anything. It's strangely comforting how little has changed.

This exercise is the reason that I didn't spend hundreds of thousands of dollars getting into debt in order to go to get an MBA that I didn't really want. It's the reason I kept writing and painting. It's the reason that I ended up in a job that is focused on tapping the potential within humans for the benefit of the organizations they work for. It's the reason that I genuinely feel that the work I do is fulfilling and brings me joy every day, because it helped me to define in concrete terms what gives versus takes away my energy. It enabled me to influence the balance of my life to limit the activities that drain me and do more of what fills me up.

How to answer this question for yourself:

This exercise is not intended to spit out your life purpose (stay with me, all you Type A neurotics who crave instant gratification), but instead structure your thinking to hone in on what brings you energy, enthusiasm and joy versus what saps those things for you. It can be used to assess a lot of different activities, including jobs, hobbies, volunteer efforts, and obligations that we get tied up in because we aren't prepared to articulate why we cannot participate.

Have you ever heard the expression that "if it isn't a hell yes, it's a no"? I used to hate that expression, because there are literally only three things on Earth that I have that kind of reaction to given my overly analytical nature. This exercise is the pragmatic version of the "hell yes" test, that will help you to get extremely clear on how to start spending your minutes, hours, days, and years in a way that is more closely aligned with your purpose. It will limit the amount of choices available to you, and serve as the "fishbowl" or framework to filter viable options that Barry Schwartz suggests we all need to be content with our decisions.

Below are the instructions. If you do this exercise right, it will take you a few hours. (If you're someone who needs more structure, you can also download a template for this exercise on my website at colleenbordeaux.com/book.)

#1 Find a quiet spot, gather three sheets of computer paper, and label the top of each page with the following: "Things I dislike," "Things I love," and "Non-negotiables."

You're going to need a total of three hours to do this exercise, and it's OK to space out each hour over a few days to give you time to reflect. If it gives you anxiety to take this kind of time for an exercise that sort of feels like homework, just remember that it's basically the time you'd spend on a long movie but instead of leaving you with guilt for how many Milk Duds you ate, it will leave you with more clarity on how to spend the rest of your life. I'd say it's worth the time.

#2 Set a timer for 60 minutes and sit with the "Things I dislike" page.

Without judgment, list every possible thing that comes to mind in that hour on your "Things I dislike" page. Consider the "shoulds" that have trailed you in life to date, where you feel like you don't belong, or don't do particularly well, or are not passionate about. These can be aspects about a job, a boss, a city, an apartment, relationships, you name it. If it kills your energy, enthusiasm, and joy, it belongs on the list.

If you feel like you can go for longer than an hour, feel free to keep writing. My list included things, such as "sitting in traffic," "being micromanaged," "laziness," "negative attitudes," "downtime and boredom," "making pivot tables," "sitting in a cubicle all day long," "talking on the phone," and "feeling like I need to fit a mold."

#3 Set that list aside, and repeat the process with the "Things I love" page.

Same as with your dislike list, absolve yourself of judgment and list every possible thing that comes to mind in that hour when you think of things that bring you joy. Think about what you're passionate about, what you would do for free, who you are engaging with, what you've achieved that you're proud of, what you've done uncommonly well, where you feel like you belong, how you're wired. If you feel like you can go for longer than an hour, feel free to keep writing.

My list included things, such as "having time to spend with [my boyfriend, now husband] every day," "interacting with positive, thoughtful people," "exploring new places," "writing," "being challenged and pushed to my limits," "feeling like the work I do matters," "hot yoga," "helping people solve their problems," "being friends with my co-workers," and "making lots of money." (She said don't apply any judgment!) When you're done, set both lists aside and take a break for a day.

"Success is no accident. It is hard work, perseverance, learning, studying, sacrifice, and, most of all, love of what you are doing or learning to do." - Pele

#3 Get a red pen, and go back through both lists to select the non-negotiables.

Ask yourself: "Is this non-negotiable, something that I know in my bones is right or wrong for me?" If yes, circle it in red pen. This is something you absolutely cannot deal with or absolutely must have in whatever you do. It's a subjective assessment, but be as honest with yourself as possible, and pay attention to how you're feeling when you're making that call.

#4 Take out your "Non-negotiables" page to summarize from both lists.

Draw a line down the center of the page. On one side, write "No" and on the other side write "Yes." Copy each of your non-negotiable items from your "dislike" list into the "No" column. Each of your non-negotiable items from your "love" list goes into the "Yes" column.

This non-negotiables page is your "purpose filter," the considered facts about the unique mix of things that light you up versus sap your joy. It's a tool to help eliminate some of the noise that tends to distract us into decisions that lead us away from our purpose.

#5 Make your transition plan.

You don't have to overhaul your life overnight, but you should have a level of urgency to start doing something every single day to create the capacity to do more of what you identified as the non-negotiables on your "Things I love" worksheet and to eliminate from your life the non-negotiables on your "Things I dislike" worksheet. It might require you to start a job search, stop doing something you've been doing forever, or take a class.

Figure out what it is that you need to change in order to start shifting the balance in favor of what brings you joy, and do it as quickly as you possibly can, because your life and time to live your purpose is literally passing you by.

Darren Hardy once said that the power of focus is like a little kid using a magnifying glass to burn a bug on a sidewalk. All of the energy of the sun is already around him, but the magnifying glass allows that energy to be focused and harnessed. The power of decision and focused action is like a magnifying glass for your energy, helping you to harness it and get the life outcomes you desire.

"If you never say no to what you don't want, you'll never have the energy for what you do want." - Darren Hardy

I took my "non-negotiables" list and applied it to the job I'd verbally accepted, and realized that it would lead me to be living many of the aspects that I'd selected as non-negotiables from my "Things I dislike" list and just a few non-negotiables from my

"Things I love" list. So, I turned the job down confidently. This non-negotiables list helped me to not only have the resolve to stick it out (for 18 months!) until I found the right fit (the firm and group that I'm still working for, years later), but has helped me to make many big, life-altering decisions to shift the balance towards things that bring me joy and enable me to give the best of myself to others.

"Your vision will become clear only when you look into your heart. Who looks outside, dreams. Who looks inside, awakens." - Carl Jung

This exercise ultimately helps you to define what makes you unique, what lights you up, and where to focus. It gives you a filter for evaluating options and making decisions, but won't be useful unless you discipline yourself to seek and develop those things that make you unique and bring joy and value to others. Don't judge yourself for what lights you up, don't let fear of what other people will think keep you from doing them, and definitely don't talk yourself into doing other things that are more practical instead.

"Discover your uniqueness, then discipline yourself to develop it." - Jim Sundberg

Making decisions and changes in your life around what you learn through this simple process is how you start to live out your purpose. As your life purpose starts to take shape in your mind, you must remember that the only thing that makes it real is you taking action!

It's the most terrifyingly humbling experience to go in the direction of your unique purpose. No one else will understand it or can do it for you. It requires you to believe in yourself and your own inner voice, to be courageous, to do things you've never done before, to start to value yourself and what you have to offer more than what your family or friends or colleagues might think.

I've found it helpful to reflect on the question, "What would eighty-year-old-me tell me to do?" I can 100 percent guarantee she'd tell me to do whatever I need to increase my capacity to exude joy, energy, enthusiasm, and positivity in the service of others. You can also try, "What would I tell my best friend or my child or someone I really love to do?" Hype yourself the way you hype those you care about to build the courage to go out and do the things that bring them joy.

Summary of the key takeaway from this chapter:

You are here to serve others with your life and with your joy. It is your responsibility to figure out what lights you up, brings you joy, and increases your energy, enthusiasm, and ability to serve others—and create the capacity to do more of whatever that is. Remember how it was your "job" to make good grades in school? Now it's your "job" to create and live a life that adds value to others in a way that brings you joy and increases your capacity to serve.

Recommended books with more research, ideas, and practical tips to answer this question:

The Paradox of Choice by Barry Schwartz
Originals by Adam Grant
The Alchemist by Paulo Coelho
The Defining Decade by Dr. Meg Jay
The Compound Effect by Darren Hardy
Start with Why by Simon Sinek
Called to Create by Jordan Raynor
How Will You Measure Your Life by Clayton Christensen

CHAPTER 3

Speaking of my meat suit, is there a user guide?

A foundation for keeping your body
healthy as long as you care to live.

Other forms of this question include thoughts, such as, "I just have bad genes," or, "I hate my body," or ,"Everyone in my family dies young, so what's the point in trying," or, "There is too much effing information about what to eat, so I'll stick with my refined sugar and MSG, thanks."

"Eat. Not too much. Mostly plants." - Michael Pollan

Before I get into writing this chapter, I just want to acknowledge that there are some haters who will say I'm not a doctor, a nutritionist or qualified at anything, and who am I to be talking to people about the care and feeding of their meat suits. (Haters gonna hate.) In fact, I *almost* didn't include this chapter because it's such a sensitive topic. As someone who has owned and cared for a meat suit for 32 years, I know it's not easy.

As much as I wish there were a supreme, highly qualified doctor-of-everything to tell us exactly what we're supposed to do, that doctor does not exist. So as owner-of-meat-suit to owner-of-meat-suit, I thought it might be refreshing to revisit the fundamentals on this topic from a non-expert point of view, because getting real about what works when it comes to managing our meat suits is an essential factor in living out our purpose in this world.

By the way, I know there are some people out there who subscribe to the whole, "I'm here for a good time, not for a long time" philosophy of life. This chapter is not for those people. If that sounds like you, this is the time to skip ahead to the next chapter. Enjoy your Cheetos. Centenarians-to-be, please continue.

Before we get any further into this topic, let's revisit what it means to be "healthy." From my perspective, it's more than simply feeling OK or not being sick or having a mediocre existence. To me, being healthy means to be full of life and energy and vitality, to be confident in the physical form that carries you around this Earth.

I'm going to go out on a limb here and suggest that eighty-year-old you doesn't want diabetes and creaky bones and a liver on dialysis. She wants to go to yoga and take salsa dancing lessons with her girlfriends and feel confident that her meat suit can carry her for another twenty-plus years.

If that sounds crazy to you, consider this: our life spans are dramatically expanding, and your odds of living past 80 are exponentially better than previous generations, according to Lynda Gratton and Andrew Scott, authors of "The 100 Year

Life," whose research suggests that a child born today has a 50 percent chance of living past the age of 100.

This lengthened timeline on Earth for millions of people begs the question of how to take advantage of those extra years instead of simply dying over the course of a couple extra decades.

There are plenty of people between the ages of 80 and 100 years old in nursing homes (or in the homes of people who have been forced to become primary caregivers because they cannot afford a nursing home for their loved ones) across the country, in wheelchairs, tied to catheters, and in an incredible amount of physical and spiritual pain.

There are also many people between the ages of 80 and 100 years old who are teaching yoga classes, giving keynote speeches and island hopping on yachts in the Caribbean. If you don't believe me, Google Tao Porchon Lynch, who is currently 100-something years old, can fold her legs behind her head and speak to groups of thousands, then jog off the stage and give Tony Robbins a high five.

Which group does your eighty-year-old self want to be in?

My point in writing those last two paragraphs is because I believe that there's a growing urgency for us all to get on board with doing a better job with caring for our meat suits and managing the controllable elements of our health, if only so our children and families won't have their joy sucked from having to care for us as we slowly decay from ailments we could have prevented through better thinking and actions today.

I don't know about you, but I want to do everything in my power to be as vivacious and energetic as possible all the way until the end. As a matter of fact, I care so much about this that I even have a vision for my own death.

It's something like this: I'm at least 122 years old, sitting in my home on a green, velvet chaise lounge in a silk, leopard dress and a giant, cashmere sweater surrounded by my very best friends and family, laughing at my own jokes and relishing in the delightful personalities I've been blessed to enjoy as we sip coffee and talk about everything and nothing all at the same time.

Out of nowhere, I say: "OK, I think I'm spent" and drop dead on the spot, not in a dramatic way with my mouth agape and limbs splayed unnaturally, but more like someone who nods off in a movie. My friends and family take my pulse and remark about how they're not surprised that I left my body like I left every party I ever attended, "Irish exiting" and then immediately falling asleep.

They pull my "funeral instructions" file out of my desk drawer, discover that I have everything planned and paid (pending date confirmation, of course), and have even written a speech that I wanted to be shared posthumously by my doppelganger great-granddaughter so my friends and family hear straight-from-the-horse's-mouth my explicit instructions to send me off with joy instead of grief, because I literally hate negativity and want them to remember me for my joie de vivre.

What, you don't have a vision for your own death? (I see you Type A planners out there nodding your heads, adding foam core posters to your Amazon Prime carts to make your death vision boards.) Anyway, where were we? Oh yes, how to take care of your meat suit over the course of your likely long life to make your death-vision a reality.

One idea I really love on meat suit care and feeding is from this 13th century philosopher named John Duns Scotus who wrote about "the harmony of goodness," which is this idea that love for the self always overflows into love for the other. Airline companies tap into this philosophy when they advise people in those boring videos to affix their own air mask before helping others. The idea is that if you do not take care of yourself, you cannot give to others. My perspective is that taking care of your meat suit is essentially love for the self that overflows into love for the other.

This is not a revolutionary idea. When I am eating right, moving my body and getting good sleep, I am a delightful blessing to everyone whose path I cross. When I am hangry, sedentary and exhausted, I have the potential to push my husband down a staircase and pretend it was an accident. [Note to editor: is it cool to include my homicidal thoughts in here?] [Response from my editor, Travis: "As long as he doesn't wind up dead from a staircase fall."]

So if the idea that taking care of your meat suit enables you to be your best, happiest self is so straightforward, why do we struggle so much with this?

Ahh, the ultimate question! There have been millions of articles and books and studies and careers built on this question alone. (Cue Barry Schwartz and the Paradox of Choice.) Beyond information overwhelm, the reasons behind why we struggle to take care of our physical selves are wide and varied, and I don't have the patience to get into the weeds on that.

According to my research on the topic, one of the primary reasons we struggle with being healthy is because we have so many effed up beliefs about health, focusing nearly all of the energy and resources on negatives like disease management instead of maintaining our health and vitality.

This isn't just my opinion: according to the Centers for Disease Control and Prevention, 95 percent of all health expenditures are related to the treatment of illness; only 5 percent is spent on prevention. According to a 2017 Global Chronic Diseases Management Market report, we've spent more than $264B on obesity and $300B on smoking related health issues. Put another way, what we spend treating just obesity and smoking-related issues is a lot more money than the gross domestic product of many, many nations.

My point is that is a ton of money spent on treating (predominantly) preventable issues. Despite all that money we spend on treating the negatives, those treatments and services we're paying for only impact around 10 percent of the factors that determine our health outcomes! The remaining ~90 percent of determinants of health are a result of genetic, behavioral, socioeconomic, and environmental causes.

Said simply, more than 90 percent of what matters in maintaining your meat suit has nothing to do with the health care system! Genetics aside (because we're stuck with those until someone figures out how to hack the genome), pretty much everything else related to keeping our meat suits healthy is under our control. That's amazing news!

Yet despite what the research suggests, we spend almost no time focusing on how to create and maintain our vitality over the course of our lives, to understand our meat suits and their unique needs, and to find the right way of caring for them that optimizes their health and longevity.

It might be because "being healthy" has become such a complex topic, driven by our collective belief system that encourages treatment and services in a traditional health care setting rather than taking a step back to consider how behavioral or environmental changes might be more effective.

Here's a short take on the challenge at hand with these "controllable factors" related to taking care of our meat suits: we live in a world where our access to calories has grown exponentially over the past fifty years—imagine that people used to survive without national restaurant chains and grocery stores in every town, and now we can get a bottle of wine and a deep-dish pizza delivered to our front door in a matter of minutes. And there are so many mixed opinions on what is or isn't "healthy" that we've just given up and gone after what tastes good. We work in jobs that keep us in tiny beige cubicles that require limited movement, and we reduce exercise to a time of day and a particular setting that doesn't feel like a fun or valuable part of our life.

We don't have the time to get into all of the complexities of the systemic issues, but here's something else to chew on (pun intended) about what may be causing us to have poor health: our food sources have dramatically changed over the past several decades, with an explosion in the variety of food we consume, as well as the added hormones and toxins that inevitably affect our bodies. Roughly fifteen million Americans manage food allergies, and a countless number deal with food intolerances and sensitivities that go undiagnosed, according to Dr. Stephen Gundry, author of "The Plant Paradox." There are also BPAs! Toxins! That whole thing about how jogging breaks down collagen!

Whew, okay, where were we? Ah yes, health. Vitality. The burning platform for change to live your best life! And how to think about taking care of your meat suit a little bit better, from a novice meat suit owner who has done a lot of research and thinking on the topic and has found a few ideas to be helpful along the way.

I struggled with those questions for a long time and have found a few simple, refreshing answers along the way that have made both much easier for me. But before I share, a personal story about my own meat suit management issues...

My personal struggle with this question:

I was raised on oatmeal, Wonder Bread sandwiches, and tuna casserole for 18 years, an efficient and cost effective meal plan for a large family and source of essential carbs to fuel my early morning swim practices during the week and compulsory yard work on weekends. The idea of weight management never entered my mind until I graduated college, moved to frigid Minneapolis, and began working in a cubicle.

On the "cube farm" at my first job, the dramatic drop in movement caught up with me quickly, and I responded to my pants getting tighter by simply eating less. At one point, I was more or less on a completely liquid diet (soup), and my boss kept offering to buy me a sandwich in line at the work cafeteria because he was worried I was starving (sorry, Nate).

When spring came, I started running at lunch and normalized my eating habits only to repeat the process the moment the temperatures dropped in the fall and my pants started to squeeze me again. It started a cycle of obsessing over my size and weight, driven by patterns of undereating and overeating, and phases of sedentary and extreme activity. When I started working in consulting, my stress and alcohol levels spiked in a powerful unison, and I responded by restricting my calories and doing ninety-minute hot yoga classes four times a week and running on the off days.

When friends and family told me I was too thin, I secretly loved it. The cycles continued to repeat, picking up steam as I learned more about how to manipulate my own body. I tried Paleo for an eight-month stretch to stay fit for my wedding while working fourteen-hour days on the road, then went into a Pad Thai all day, every day phase after my honeymoon. My friends taught me about cutting carbs, juicing, and cleansing, which I tried with gusto only to get back to a place where I was so confused on what to eat that I just gave up until my pants felt tight again, and I went back to the drawing board to learn about metabolism hacking and fasting and HIIT (high-intensity interval training).

Once, I literally Googled this exact phrase: "How to stay fit when you work fourteen-hour days, hate exercise, and love wine and chocolate" and, shockingly, found no credible ideas. The years of stress, alcohol consumption, unhealthy eating patterns and limited exercise finally caught up to me in a much bigger way that I couldn't manipulate through diet and exercise. It came in the form of a horrible bout of inflammatory issues, the most pronounced being a case of fiery rosacea marked by blisters all over my cheeks that no makeup could conceal and a level of bloat and weight gain that did not respond to my usual tactics no matter how little I ate or how much I exercised. My dermatologist told me my options were to go on a low-dose antibiotic for perpetuity, or deal with the root cause. "Tell me more," I said.

She referred me to a naturopathic doctor, who interviewed me about my life and tested my blood for hormone imbalances, environmental allergens, and food intolerances. He sat me down with the results, a heat map of a wide range of foods that my body struggled to process—things like rice, wheat, and basil.

He explained that I had candidiasis, an overgrowth of yeast in the gut that was directly linked to the rosacea and the other inflammatory issues I had (as well as to all of the sugar and alcohol I was consuming).

Although I was desperate for a quick cleanse or a pill, he told me the only way to cure what I was struggling with was to completely overhaul my diet. He outlined a ninety-day elimination plan that cut sugar, alcohol, and all of the foods I'd developed sensitivities to and recommended a diet of almost entirely organic and unprocessed foods, heavy on fresh vegetables, legumes, fruit, nuts and lean protein along with supplements to support hormone balance.

During this process, I was told that I also had to work on better managing my stress response on a day-to-day basis, because the cortisol spikes were not doing me any favors. It forced me to take stock of myself and my lifestyle, and get creative on what I could realistically do with the limited time and motivation I had to exercise.

The only way I could consistently exercise was hiring a personal trainer for Saturday mornings, pre-booking Sunday hot yoga classes, and releasing myself from the pressure of trying to squeeze in workouts Monday through Friday. Instead, I simply made the commitment to get up and walk around every 45 minutes, stand whenever I could, and listen to my beloved podcasts while walking (which I dubbed "TEDwalks," trademark pending).

I came out on the other side with the best skin and energy levels of my life, and also in the best shape of my life even though I was not trying nearly as hard on the exercise front. It was shocking, because it flew in the face of everything I'd been told about eating well and moving my body.

I'm telling you all of this because I think it's important to recognize that we all struggle with this loaded topic in different ways, and I think it's because we've been fed a lot of garbage (literally and figuratively) that distracts us from really knowing our meat suits and taking care of them in a way that works for us.

On top of everything we covered earlier in this chapter about how our health care system focuses on treating negative outcomes instead of maintaining vitality, how our food sources are rife with stuff that isn't good for our bodies, it's compounded by the fact that we live in a culture that seems to consistently communicate that being thin and beautiful is a qualification for being loved, which puts all of us somewhere on the spectrum of falling short, staring at our thigh gaps or lack thereof, setting goals for weights or dress sizes, and picking apart our meat suits for every flaw we can find.

It's genius, actually, because we'll go to almost any length and expense to "fix" our meat suits, which is so great for the diet and exercise industry. You've got a pill, an app, a machine that can fix me? Where do I swipe?! (If you don't relate in any way to this, please contact me to rewrite this chapter and maybe whole book because you've cracked the code and together we're going to make millions.)

Because I struggled so much in this area, I've learned that there is a happy medium between accepting your meat suit for everything that it is, giving up on changing it, and living on exclusively fried food and sugar, versus defining areas where it's not as healthy and energetic and life-giving as possible and changing how you care for it in a way that you can sustain over the course of your life.

That place is different for each of us, but it exists. I'm pleased to report that I have found that happy medium for myself, and the effect it's had on my confidence and life overall is astounding. It involved getting to know the facts about what my own body needs versus doesn't tolerate, and defining for myself what the right amount of movement looks like at this stage of my life.

Finding that happy medium point—and letting go of anything that makes me feel negative about my meat suit (including all fitspo, scales, etc.)—has made it incredibly simple to maintain. If I step outside of that happy medium point of how I eat and move in order to enjoy a party or a vacation, I don't let myself feel guilty—I simply step back into it the next day.

This took me an incredibly long time to learn, involving a lot of self-reflection and research. I think if everyone knew that they could define their own happy medium point for taking care of their meat suit, we'd put entire industries out of business and Tuscany would be really crowded with old drunk people on unicycles in eighty years. (Did I sell you on Tuscany yet? Because I'm definitely getting kickbacks for this. Just kidding, I'm not, but I should. cc: Tuscany Board of Tourism.)

How to answer this question for yourself:

#1 Appreciate your body and everything it does for you.

For me, I appreciate that my body is free of diseases, that it is strong, resilient and harbors a good immune system that keeps me from catching colds or the flu despite all the time I spend on planes. It is literally a machine that runs on autopilot, save for the occasional food and water inputs it requires. I love that it lights up after yoga or a long walk and has the capacity to morph and change to fix a cut or heal a zit or grow back a bad haircut or create new life.

Your meat suit is miraculous! It is a gift! Remembering that will make it much, much easier to talk to it nicely and to treat it like you would want your daughter or best friend to treat their meat suits. Plus, how you feel about your body has physiological ramifications on your health. Did you know that the trillions of cells in your body literally work nonstop and are under the command of your mind? So your thoughts, feelings, and beliefs inevitably impact how those cells operate. Don't believe me?

Google what happens when you laugh—it's a thought that triggers a physical response in your body.

Scientists at the Institute of HeartMath have shown that feelings of love, gratitude, and appreciation (in general, but also for your meat suit specifically) boost your immune system, increase vital chemicals production, reduce stress hormone levels, and improve glucose regulation.

"Your emotions affect every cell in your body. Mind and body, mental and physical, are intertwined." - Thomas Tutko

#2 Understand the facts about how your body operates.

Get the facts about your body beyond just weight and BMI—they get way too much focus. Get your blood tested for hormone imbalances that might be standing in your way or food intolerances and sensitivities that might be causing downstream issues in your body. Track what you consume and how your body responds to it. Experiment and make changes as you learn what gives you energy versus slows you down.

#3 Determine your healthy weight and stop thinking about it.

If you don't already know this, talk to your doctor or do the research on how to calculate your ideal weight. Make a decision to get to and stick with that "set point," and then stop thinking about it. If you're addicted to your scale or it makes you feel bad, find a different way to monitor it. Scales make me crazy, so I don't use them. Haven't stepped on one in more than a year, I go by how my clothes feel, period, and I've completely stopped obsessing over the numbers.

#4 Do the work to cure yourself of addictions to the stuff that your body struggles with.

Most of us know what these are, but if you're not sure then see a nutritionist or dietician or get the blood tests mentioned in point #2. My body gets addicted to sugar incredibly easily and doesn't handle it well. A few days of holiday treats will lead me to headaches and cravings for weeks afterwards. Cutting sugar out of my diet completely is the only way that I can control it. Maybe for you it's caffeine, or wheat, or salt, or something else. Or maybe you're lucky enough not to have addictions to things that your body does better without.

#5 Fuel your body with primarily the things that it thrives on, and avoid as much as possible the things it struggles with.

One of the best pieces of advice that I ever received regarding healthy eating to focus on adding in healthy foods rather than subtracting things from my diet. Although I did subtract stuff per my food sensitivities mentioned above, thinking about what I need more of has helped me to stay focused.

When I think about needing at least one serving of healthy fat or protein, and focus on having vegetables and greens covering at least half of my plate, I give my body those things first and there are simply fewer opportunities and less appetite to impulsively consume things that it doesn't handle well. I keep avocados on my countertop, individually wrapped packets of olives and pistachios in my purse, leafy greens in my fridge, and frozen broccoli florets and cauliflower rice in my freezer, so I always have something on hand to meet my "must-eat" requirements and avoid bringing the things my body reacts to poorly into the house. (Except for Papa John's pizza, because my husband cannot be controlled.)

#6 Find a way to move your body that you genuinely enjoy.

If you dread going to the gym and hate running, you shouldn't force yourself to do those things. We only have so much time on this Earth, and if our purpose is to serve others with our joy, exercise in a way that lights you up. I used to drag myself to spin classes, the hotel gym, and outside to jog. It always felt like punishment, and I was never able to stick with it. Reframing exercise as an activity I enjoy that requires movement changed the game for me. I love going to see my personal trainer and to hot yoga, or taking my dog on a long walk while listening to a great podcast, or putting wine in a tumbler and walking with my husband or a friend.

#7 Outline a strategy based on the routines and common scenarios for your lifestyle.

In her amazing book, "Lean for Life," Louise Parker talks about the mental framework she uses when it comes to her health. She has an "inner circle" where she spends most of her time, eating the foods that serve her body, avoiding what doesn't, and moving in the way that her body needs. She also has an "outer circle" that is composed of vacations and dinners out with friends and other scenarios where she "steps out" of her normal "inner circle" pattern of eating and movement for a bit, and then simply steps right back into the "inner circle" when the "outer circle" event is over. Louise calls it a dance, and I love it because it's such a healthy, guilt-free way to think about how we eat and move.

So define your "inner circle" and what it looks like in the common scenarios of your life: when you're cooking at home on the weekends, working long hours during the week, attending family dinners, and so on. Because I travel so much, my "inner circle" has variations of what I make myself when I am home, as well as what I purchase and eat on the road. If I am heading to O'Hare on a Monday morning, I know exactly what I'm picking up for my breakfast and will be "that girl" who customizes *literally everything* about her meal at the restaurant in order to stay in my "inner circle" (special shout out to PF Changs by the West End Marriott in Nashville, who used to make me the most boring meal of sauce-free steamed broccoli and plain broiled chicken, no questions asked).

Summary of the key takeaway from this chapter:

Your meat suit is your vehicle for living out your purpose in this world, and it is meant to be vivacious, full of energy, and a tool for you to radiate the light that you were born to give others. It is your responsibility to take care of the meat suit you were given in the best way that you can, by learning what makes it tick, by listening to what it needs, by giving it the fuel it deserves for working so hard to carry you all over this Earth, by taking it for walks and stretches and telling it that you're proud of it and you appreciate how much it does for you, and treating it in a way that reflects that level of gratitude.

Recommended books with more research, ideas, and practical tips to answer this question:

Lean for Life by Louise Parker
Always Hungry by Daniel Ludwig
The Plant Paradox by Dr. Stephen Gundry
How Not to Die by Dr. Michael Greger
The 4-Hour Body by Tim Ferriss
Younger by Harold Lancer
Younger Skin Starts in the Gut by Nigma Talib

CHAPTER 4

How do I control the blob of cho- lesterol that tells me what to do?

An orientation to mind control

Other forms of this question include constant rumination over things that happened in the past, persistent anxiety over things that might happen in the future, and uncontrollable thoughts that are gonna do what they are gonna do—just like Donald Trump's Twitter thumbs.

"No one can produce great things who is not thoroughly sincere in dealing with himself." - James Russell Lowell

Oh hello, welcome to the chapter on mind control! We've touched on the topic of mind control in the previous chapters when it comes to drowning out negative self-talk and channeling our higher selves. This chapter is going to delve more deeply into the power of our minds in creating our thoughts, behaviors, decisions, and, ultimately, life outcomes.

I believe it is the second-most important chapter in this entire book. After you find out who the eff you are, it's incredibly important to learn how to dance the fine line between self-acceptance and self-development, and put in the work to grow yourself for the better by controlling your own mind instead of letting it control you.

There's a lot to be said about this fine line between self-acceptance and self-development, and how we tend to go too far in either direction. On one hand, accepting yourself and your flaws and the whole shebang is great. Me and my big nose and my bony toes and my neuroses are just fine; we love us, thanks. It's not great when it becomes an excuse for letting character flaws run wild. I literally cannot stand it when people say, "This is just who I am" as an excuse for bad behavior. Oh, really? You're just rude and late and selfish and judgmental and impatient and unkind, and that's never going to change?

"Every day you spend working on yourself to be better than you were yesterday isn't only for you but the betterment of everyone around you." - Rachel Wolchin

On the other hand, self-development can go too far when it's taken beyond growing your mind and character to the point where you're so focused on what you have to fix that it becomes a distraction, or a crutch, or a mission and drives insecurity or self-loathing, rather than a tool that is helpful and leading to growth.

Accepting yourself for who you are means to rest in the confidence that your higher, innately worthy self that we talked about in the first chapter is inherently valuable and enough, to let go of your pain and past mistakes, and trust that the Universe or God or whatever form of higher intelligence you may subscribe to will provide everything you need—if you allow this higher self to guide you. It does not mean that you don't have to learn from your mistakes or admit when you're wrong or look at your own thoughts and behaviors with a critical eye to suss out where you may have some character flaws that need to be addressed.

So now that we've gotten that out of the way, the remainder of this chapter will focus on how to control your mind to improve your own character, expand your thinking, and channel your higher self to drive the outcomes you want in life. But before we dig in, I want to put some context around the power of our minds and the way in which we use our thoughts to create our life outcomes. People don't realize that our minds are literally an incredibly powerful, creative force, and I am going to get *really extra* in making sure you understand that before you leave this chapter.

A quick aside on quantum physics and the creative power of your mind:

I believe, thanks to many quantum physicists who have shared their research and theories on this topic (special shoutout to my ultimate crush, Richard Feynman) that we are each a microcosm of the entire universe, meaning that the human body is made up of the same fundamental particles, principles and laws that make up the entire universe. A similar idea is also found in religious contexts.

For example, in the Greek Orthodox Church, the idea of deification, that a person is a microcosm of God created in order to participate in the divinity of God, is something that I personally find inspiring when I consider what I've learned about mind control and how that potentially translates to my Catholic understanding of the Holy Spirit. Another example can be found in Asian traditions that believe the body of a human being is a mini-cosmos, a reflection of the larger cosmos in which we live.

Anyway, back to quantum physics because people tend to trust science as a framework, so we'll just go with that one for now. The idea that we're each mini-reflections of the universe is best understood in thinking about the universe as an ocean, and we're each a drop of water within that ocean, separate entities made of the same substance and operating under the same set of principles and laws.

OK, so now that you hopefully with me on the humans-as-microcosms point, I'll sum up the rest of this highly complex theory in a run-on sentence or two. We can all agree that there are laws we accept about our universe that govern what happens. Cue Sir Isaac Newton getting hit in the head with an apple and the Wright brothers making the first successful flight as examples when humans have applied and tested the universal laws of gravity and physics, which we now accept as fact, because we view science as objective and measurable.

Another example I love is Marconi, a guy whose own friends locked him up in a mental institution because he wouldn't shut up about his idea that there were these ethers floating around in the air that he could channel to send messages. Marconi escaped from the psych ward and invented the radio, which changed the course of human history.

My point is, once discovered and tested, these scientific laws are accepted as real but everyone thought they were batsh*t crazy before that. Many highly intelligent people believe that the human constructs we use to understand scientific laws are imperfect and that other universal laws exist that we either haven't discovered, don't have the capacity to understand, or can't measure and test. Philosophers love this stuff, the idea that there are vapors of universal laws dictating outcomes that our feeble human brains can't even begin to grasp.

Some schools of thought argue that certain measurable, commonly accepted universal laws like gravity represent much broader universal laws that govern outcomes of our thinking and behavior. For example, the laws governing positive and negative magnetics in science could be related to our human framework of understanding right and wrong in philosophy, or good and evil in religion.

Simply put, our human frameworks of understanding that we call science, philosophy, and religion could be all talking about exactly the same thing. Are you still with me, or did I just take us way too far into the quantum physics wormhole?

The reason I brought quantum physics into this (besides the fact that it is the genius, hipster cousin of science and makes me sound *very educated*) is because this entire chapter on mind control is based on the following assumptions:

#1 That we live in an inherently creative universe with some sort of law that ties positive / right / moral energy to positive / right / moral outcomes, and has the exact opposite effect for negative / wrong / evil energy, and...

#2 That each of us, as scientifically proven micro-reflections of the substance, principles, and laws of the universe, are inherently creative beings with the capacity for both positive / right / moral and negative / wrong / evil through how we channel our thoughts and produce outcomes in our lives.

"Always seek to conquer myself rather than fortune, to change my desires rather than established order, and gen-

erally to believe that nothing except our thoughts is wholly under our control so that after we have done our best in external matters, what remains to be done is absolutely impossible, as least as far as we are concerned." - Rene Descartes

The idea that we have the capacity for tremendous good, or positivity, to live up to our full potential and use our unique perspectives and talents to serve the world is a common fabric among many of the world religions, which focus on the concept of free will or choice in how we think and act. When I hear the words "good" and "evil," my mind conjures an image of Mother Teresa for the former and Hitler for the latter—both symbols that seem very far off from my own life and capacities.

But if we were to go back to that philosophical idea that the capacity for good or evil is simply a loaded way of saying that we have the capacity to create positive energy or negative energy through our thoughts, it suddenly becomes very tangible.

My hypothesis is that allowing your instinctually negative animal mind run the show dramatically increases your odds of being the kind of person that creates negative outcomes and sucks joy from other people, and consciously tuning in to your higher self allows you to nip any of those animal brain negative thoughts in the bud and replace them with more productive, creative, value-added thoughts.

"A man who is master of himself can end a sorrow as he can invent a pleasure. I don't want to be at the mercy of my emotions. I want to use them, to enjoy them, and to dominate them." - Oscar Wilde

I know what you're thinking. What do you do if you haven't tuned into your higher self, if you can't find him or her? The answer is that you need to spend some time inside your own head and find the voice. It's in there, giving you mad props for reading this book and yelling to be heard over your animal brain. Sometimes you may have heard it quietly say things like, "It's been a while since you've called Mom" or, "I really hope Sally can't hear this conversation because she would be really hurt."

I hate it when people say, "She's so in her head" or, "Get out of your head" because 1) that presumes you're just ruminating in loops of unproductive thought, which I totally get that a lot people do (I used to be one of them), but doing serious critical thinking is a good thing and requires one to be in one's head and 2) literally everything happens in your head, and you've gotta be in there to control that giant blob of cholesterol or it will ruin your life!

Marcus Aurelius famously stated that "our life is what our thoughts make it." You can control your thoughts to make the life you want, or you can let them control you and end up with regrets.

Consider Anwar el Sadat, former president of Egypt. Very long story short, Anwar used to be a real a-hole and spent a lot of time talking about how much he wanted to wipe Israel off the face of the Earth, inciting rage and violence across the region. He was basically the Arab Spring's worst nightmare and a real rock in the shoes of several world leaders at the time, including Russia and America. Today he is an international symbol of peace.

You know how he went from being a terrifying, trigger-happy demon on the nightly news to a respected world leader who called for the end of all wars?

You might have surmised by now that he didn't do it by blowing Israel off the face of the Earth. No sir, no ma'am. He did an about-face, shifting from an extreme focus on negative, unproductive thinking aiming to gain control and influence over others, to an extreme focus on positive, productive thinking aiming to gain control and influence over his own mind. And he won a Nobel Peace Prize for it and literally served as an example to the world for getting your head right and tuning into your higher self.

It's not easy to do, mind you, even for someone whose negative thought patterns have not led them to call for the annihilation of an entire nation on international television.

Your animal brain is programmed to avoid being eaten by lions, or excluded from the pack that hunts together to survive, so it instinctually operates through a negative lens to keep you safe and just like everyone else. It's the one that says things like, "This is dumb, I am dumb, everyone will make fun of me, I could lose my job" and results in you talking yourself right out of a creative thought before you even fully formulated it.

Your animal brain, without your higher self, would let fear run wild—a great strategy for ending up in Bronnie Ware's book about regrets of the dying. Negative thinking will keep you living a small, sad life of regrets—and the only way to overcome it is to take control of your own mind by tuning in to your higher self.

How to do this, you ask? I am so excited for you because this is the most fun exercise of the whole book, truly mind-blowing and life-changing if you really commit to it. And quite frankly, you have absolutely nothing to lose but the time, so humor me and give it a shot. But first let me share a personal story about how I learned this.

My personal struggle with this question:

All I know is my own mind, and I know there's a mean streak in that animal brain of mine. One that I have to keep in check.

It's insecure, judgmental, impatient, rude, dismissive, and self-ish. I used to let it totally run my life, and it caused some serious issues. It got to the point where it was so out of control it almost ruined my career.

Very long story short, I'd spent many months on a huge and perpetually delayed technology project where millions of dollars were on the line, all the leaders were tense, and practically everyone on the project team cried on the way to the airport on Monday mornings. Well, maybe not everyone, but I definitely did. I'd get home at 10 pm on Thursdays, pick a fight with my husband, silently rage on conference calls every Friday, and wouldn't be fully recovered until Saturday, only to turn around and repeat the process. I was extremely negative and am pretty sure that my entire team hated being around me and my unbridled anxiety and despair.

Two things helped me take back control of my mind, and I am going to tell you what those things were, and then explain how you can repeat them for yourself:

#1: I learned that I could control my thoughts.

A friend who could see that I was slowly losing it recommended I read Eckhart Tolle's "The Power of Now." Tolle argued that most of us focus on things we literally cannot control: we wind ourselves up over things that happened in the past that we can't change, or we worry about hypothetical situations in the future that we cannot possibly influence. I learned that the only things we can actually control are our minds and our actions in the present moment—and there's an incredible relief that comes with letting go of trying to control anything else.

#2: I realized that I was the problem.

After a few rounds of interviews to escape my project, a rival firm offered me an extremely generous job offer. Tempted to take it, I went to one of my mentors at the firm for advice. She pointed out that I could leave, join the new firm, get on a new project, and run into the exact same situation. Her advice made me realize that running away wasn't going to resolve the root issue. Armed with the painful self-awareness that I was causing my own misery, I turned down the job offer, began reading every book ever written on the topic of mindset management, and started to do the work to control my own negative thinking.

You should have seen it. My critical, frustrated, gossipy self, who used to keep a special archive file of a certain senior manager's rude emails, suddenly started to listen more, say less, assume positive intent, give others the benefit of the doubt, admit fault, and give admiration and appreciation like it was going out of style. And the results were astounding!

I still have to work on controlling my negative thinking. Just the other day I caught myself judging a girl on Instagram, literally saying to myself that she was dumb, secretly jealous of her for having an amazing business, beautiful home and happy marriage when I was in a hotel room and just had a little tiff with my husband about who the heck was going to clear time on Friday for the cleaning service to come and collect the 362,848,462 empty LaCroix cans all over our house.

And then my higher self stepped in and was like, "Oh, hey insecure Colleen who doesn't really feel good about herself right now! I see you! Get it together, because you're too smart to think like this. Remember how boring and dumb negative thinking is? Stop it. Toss that Instagram lady a nice comment and go think about how wonderful your life is."

My higher self is super bossy. The more I've learned to listen to her, the better my life has become. She chimed in when I was starting to get stressed and overwhelmed at work the other day, irrationally blaming my colleagues in my head for something stupid. "Oh girl, you did not just go there! Who are you to criticize? Are you 'Little Miss Perfect Attention To Detail' in all your presentations? Remember that email you reviewed 100 times and sent to a million important clients with the subject line "Thank"? Take a deep breath, sniff some of that lavender essential oil I know you keep in your purse to calm yo'self down, and send a nice email to every single person on your team telling them specifically why you need and appreciate them."

Today, my colleagues are surprised when I tell them I used to be a Negative Nancy who drained people. I love my higher self, and I'm so grateful to her for keeping my silly animal brain at bay when I'm at my low points, or I would literally never get anything accomplished because technically they do all the hard work and can leave me at any time.

How to answer this question for yourself:

#1 Start looking at your own mind objectively.

If you've studied philosophy, theology, or biology, you probably already know that our human ability to think about our own thoughts is one of the highest forms of intelligence we have to tap. Anyone can do it. Most people don't. Imagine pressing pause on your active mind and stepping out of it for a moment to take a look around. What negative thoughts would you find in mid-float? Maybe judgment? Or frustration?

We all have negative thoughts, and we can't stop them from popping up. Starting to train yourself to recognize those negative thoughts the moment they enter your mind allows you to start controlling them. And shifting away from negative to positive thinking is the most important factor in effective mind control.

#2 Pick one particular negative thought that tends to recur in your mind and start to actively practice redirecting it.

If I were doing this all over again, I'd start with judgment. Judgment blocks open-mindedness, creativity, empathy, confidence, and a whole host of the non-cognitive skills we need in order to maximize our life outcomes. When you feel the twinge of judgment pop up in the back of your mind, consider what that thought says about you.

Ask yourself these questions: Is there something about this person or idea that scares me, that threatens my ego? What might I not know, or understand, about this person or idea that is causing me to shut them down?

Questioning your own instinct to judge the moment it kicks in allows you to remain open, so you can choose higher thoughts and exhibit better behaviors. If you practice actively redirecting this negative thought enough, it will become a habit. You can literally rewire your brain and help your higher self out. The more you do this, the easier it becomes.

#3 Test your power to channel your own positive thoughts in the context of your day-to-day life

One of the greatest powers of positive thinking is that it gives us the ability to influence the thoughts and behaviors of other people to produce better outcomes.

Consider the situations where your negative thinking is triggered and how it might impact the people around you, and outline the alternate thoughts and behaviors that you will hold yourself accountable to in order to produce better outcomes, both in your own actions and through the responses you generate in other people. There have been a few great books on this that describe the common scenarios where most people get stuck in their negative thinking and limit their potential to connect and influence. My favorite is "How to Win Friends and Influence People" by Dale Carnegie.

The common scenarios he shares in that book and how to think differently about them are the exact ones that I studied, practiced, and benefited from in my own life and still use today. You can download a summary of these scenarios and how to think differently in each one of them to produce better outcomes on my website at colleenbordeaux.com/book.

Summary of the key takeaway from this chapter:

You are not your mind. You have an amazing ability to think about your own thoughts and redirect them to create the life that your eighty-year-old self would be proud of you for living. This means that not only do you have the ability to control your mind, you also have a responsibility to control your mind, and it is the only way that you can improve yourself and your life. If you don't control your mind, it will control you and continue to create completely avoidable self-induced problems and poor life outcomes through its impulsive, uncontrolled negative thinking.

Recommended books with more research, ideas, and practical tips to answer this question:

Essentialism by Greg McKeown
The Servant by James C. Hunter
The Power of Now by Eckhart Tolle
15 Invaluable Laws of Growth by John C. Maxwell
How to Win Friends and Influence People by Dale Carnegie
Awaken the Giant Within by Tony Robbins

CHAPTER 5

Who the eff are these people?

A fundamental truth about the power of the company you keep

Other forms of this question include thoughts, such as, "I really want to say no to being a bridesmaid, because it will be an abusive experience sure to drain my bank account, but we've been friends for years and I'm afraid I will hurt her feelings" or, "My family is so effed up, and it depresses me to receive the Williams Sonoma holiday catalog, because we will never have a beautiful Thanksgiving filled with joy, and I literally can't this year."

"You are the same today that you are going to be in five years except for two things: the people with whom you associate, and the books you read." - Charles Jones

You guys, don't hate me, but I'm going to bring Bronnie Ware back into this because two of the top five regrets of the dying in her book are related to relationships. The second-most common regret she heard was, "I wish I hadn't worked so hard," because it came at the cost of spending time with loved ones, and "I wish I had stayed in touch with my friends," which is pretty obvious.

As we discussed in Chapter 2, "Why am I running around in this meat suit?" relationships with other human beings wandering around Earth are what give our lives meaning. They create the web in which we seek inspiration and growth, as well as share our light and help us to become the best version of ourselves. But there's a condition to this that we don't do a great job of addressing: we have to thoughtfully create this web for ourselves.

Let me say that again: It is entirely your responsibility to develop and grow a web of high-quality relationships that helps you serve the world with your gifts and talents. And it's getting harder than ever to do that, for a number of complex reasons.

George Will of the Washington Post recently published a thought-provoking article on the loneliness epidemic in this country, dubbing it our number one public health crisis with physical and medical ramifications beyond being a driver of the pervasive mental health disorders of our day (i.e., depression, anxiety, etc.).

For example, "persistent loneliness" is more dangerous to longevity than often-cited causes of death, like heavy drinking and obesity, reducing average life span more than twice and three times as much, respectively. According to researchers at Brigham Young University, the impact of loneliness has comparable physical ramifications to smoking fifteen cigarettes a day and contributes to cognitive decline, including the rapid onset of Alzheimer's disease.

Opinions on causes of this loneliness epidemic cite the usual suspects: throwing out facts about how Americans check their phones every 4.3 minutes, about how the number of times

Americans entertained at home has declined almost 50 percent over the last twenty-five years, how technology has disrupted every aspect of our lives, especially how we interact with other human beings, etc.

My point is, people are literally dying of despair at an increasing clip, and no one seems to have yet figured out how to fill the hole that millions feel in their lives. And I am sure that the factors cited in the paragraph above play into the cause—along with potentially thousands of other variables that are compounding the situation. But the silver lining that I think needs to be called out here is that there are literally millions of people looking for the same kind of quality, life-giving relationships that you might be looking for, too.

As someone who has gone through periods of extreme loneliness in life, let me be the first to say that it's not easy to craft a web of life-giving relationships. We can't control the families we're born into or do much about them for the first eighteen years of our lives, and our process for making friends and maintaining friendships is pretty much established in kindergarten and never revisited. We also don't tend to put deep thought into the cultural pressures that drive our decisions related to relationships. Said simply, we leave one of the most important factors in our life fulfillment almost entirely to chance and external influence. Instead of being surrounded by only authentic relationships where we feel seen and understood and inspired to share our light, we're often surrounded by those who make us feel the opposite.

"You're the average of the five people you spend the most time with" - Jim Rohn

And that, my friends, is a far more powerful driver of loneliness than how many times you check your smartphone. If you have ever been in the company of other people and felt entirely alone, like you'd rather be home in bed, you know what I am talking about. Allowing people in your life who have succumbed to their own negative thinking is a really effective way of keeping yourself living well beneath your potential. These people have a terrible affliction which is commonly referred to as "crab mentality" by enlightened* people (*us).

Crab mentality refers to a pattern of behavior in crabs when they're trapped in a bucket. Although it would be relatively easy for any and all of the crabs to escape, any single crab that attempts to crawl out gets dragged back into the bucket by the rest of the group. It's an analogy used to explain the way of thinking best described by the phrase, "If I can't have it, neither can you."

It's hard enough to take control of how you talk to yourself, and it's next to impossible when you have crabs trying to drag you down. Unfortunately, those sad crab-people are everywhere, feeling sorry for themselves and sprinkling negativity wherever they go in order to infect everyone else.

When E.E. Cummings wrote (in my favorite poem of all time that I have now referenced at least three times) that "to be nobody but yourself in a world which does its best, day and night, to make you everyone else, is to fight the hardest battle any human being can fight and never stop fighting," he was talking about how defeating it can be when you're trying to tune in to your inner voice, and you can barely hear it because of all the loudmouthed people rattling off lists of reasons you shouldn't believe in yourself because they've never tried it themselves.

"Don't let the behavior of others destroy your inner peace."
- Dalai Lama

These crab-people can be in the form of family members, or long-time friends, or colleagues, or spouses, or impossibly perfect people you don't know but who make you feel like you're not enough in some way. They probably don't even realize that they're doing it, and may even have your best intentions at heart. But the reality is that negative, fearful thinking cannot help us to grow, and people who allow those kinds of thoughts to take hold in their own minds have the power to hold us back simply by influencing the way we think. The key is to eliminate or reduce time spent with these crab-people as much as humanly possible to create space for the amazing, life-giving relationships you need.

It's funny how intentionally seeking personal growth can make you let go of people you thought you couldn't and attract so many others who can expand your world in the best possible ways.

"It's the people we hardly know, and not our closest friends, who will improve our lives most dramatically." - Dr. Meg Jay

I know what you're thinking: "But Colleen! Does this mean I need to cut my mom or my spouse or my longtime friend out of my life?!" The reality is that I cannot answer that for you, but I will tell you that you can make some dramatic changes in how you allocate your time and attention that creates space and allows good relationships to flourish in your life. And I'm willing to bet that if you have the courage to do that, you will call the crabs in your life to attention and possibly influence them for the better.

If we want to solve for our own diseases of disconnection, it's time to stop allowing our time and attention to be dominated by mediocre relationships and start proactively investing in the critical few. It's time to take steps to make sure the top five people you spend the most time with are truly the ones that are helping you to grow and expand your life in ways that you need. If this topic makes you uncomfortable, that might be a sign that you've got some crabs on your hands that need to be dealt with in a way that does not include making yourself smaller in their presence.

Having relationships with people who help you tap into your light is critical, and eliminating those who take it away is equally as important. Consider this question: What kind of people do I need in my life that can help me get where I'm going, or benefit from what I have to share? We'll unpack how to do just that with the relationships in your life right now, covering family (which includes the one you are born into and the one you create for yourself), friendships (which includes both personal and professional), and everyone else in the world that your presence briefly touches. But first, I'd like to share a personal story.

My personal struggle with this question:

I grew up in a pretty typical suburban family, in a well-to-do suburb with a stay-at-home mom, nightly family dinners, summers at the lake, etc. There were essentially no problems in my life save for the aforementioned giant red church bus, unfortunate haircuts, and socially unacceptable hobbies. Anyway, my family situation become tumultuous almost overnight when I was 16 years old and my older brother went off the deep end in what can only be described as "latent computer genius becomes deranged drug addict."

Our ho-hum life turned upside-down as my brother bounced between hospitals, mental institutions, jail, rehab centers, halfway houses, and his old bedroom. Meanwhile, the rest of us went to family therapy at eight o'clock on Saturday mornings, dwelled on our brother's latest dramas during our daily family dinners, and rehearsed what to say when asked about how he was doing. A dark, perpetual cloud descended on our family and clung to each of us in different ways.

I'd find my mom sitting alone in the dark with his baby book on her lap, crying silently. My dad stopped sleeping. They clamped down on their conservatism and Catholicism and devoted themselves to saving my brother, honing a Pavlovian ability to recite the parable of the prodigal son any time one of us questioned my brother's dubious attempts at recovery.

Needless to say, it ceased to be a positive, life-giving environment. I went away to college, which made it easier, save for the dull guilt I felt for leaving my younger siblings to fend for themselves in the ceaseless, cyclical crusade to save our brother. Every time I called my parents or came home for the winter and summer breaks in courses, there was some new twist to the saga. I'd arrive to a house surrounded in police, or find my brother unconscious and gasping for air in his bedroom, or listen to my mom tally the thousands spent on rehab for his recovery.

I'd discover his latest crimes printed in the local paper, or watch him wheeled out of the house on a stretcher, or find him sitting at the kitchen table with dull, glassy eyes that couldn't focus. I spent a good chunk of my early adult years angry at my parents for allowing my older brother's drug addiction to become the epicenter of our family dynamic, and truly believing in the depths of my soul that everything would be better if he were dead.

My goal in graduating was to take a job that would get me out of Chicago and away from my family. Right before Christmas my senior year, my parents told us that our brother was moving back in after his latest stint at rehab was done. I was devastated. That very day, I decided to accept a job offer that would take me to Minneapolis and also booked a four-week-long solo backpacking trip to Europe before the break was over to occupy my time between graduation and my start date.

I know that I'm not supposed to say this, but I knew that if I stayed near my family, the negativity, drama, anger and sadness would hold me back in life. I'd call my parents and insist that we not talk about my brother, which they eventually respected. I'd visit for controlled periods of time, mentally preparing in advance, so I could roll with whatever drama was unfolding and then escape back to the psychological safety of my own city.

The reason I am telling you all of this is because I know how hard it can be to deal with toxic or negative relationships in your own family, to decide that you will no longer tolerate those relationships in your life, to put boundaries on interactions with people you love, and to walk away from a relationship with a family member completely. Looking back more than ten years later, it was the most important decision I ever made for my own growth and created the necessary space to build a healthier relationship with my parents and my brother, who is currently rebuilding his own life in Minneapolis, of all places.

The thing about family is that even though you inherit it and it has a huge influence on your life, it's capacity to have an effect on you only extends to the point where you're able to recognize your own threshold for what you can tolerate, and then summon the courage to assert the boundaries you need to grow.

It's the hardest to do with family, but the rule applies to everyone in your life. I think because I had to go through this experience with family, it helped me to develop a good sense for who will help make me better versus who will lead me astray in all of the relationships in my life.

"[In developed nations] the great poverty is the poverty of genuine friendship. We need friends who help to make us whole, not friends who add to our dividedness. A true friend is one who helps you to become a-better-version-

of-yourself, one who encourages you and challenges you, one who listens to you but also holds you accountable."
- Matthew Kelly

The beautiful and amazing thing about asserting boundaries and eliminating or avoiding the crab-people is that your time, energy, and spirit is saved to invest in the positive, life-giving relationships that help you live out your purpose in the world. I have been blessed with wonderful friends who have become family to me, helping me to push through challenging times and periods of self-doubt, who have cried with me and laughed with me and helped me to find perspective when I didn't know where to look. I have been fortunate to work with brilliant people who pushed me to step up my game, to think differently, to get out of my comfort zone, and who have helped me to become smarter and better.

Forgive me for getting sappy, but every single one of these positive, life-giving relationships have helped to shape me and grow me into the person I am right now, sitting here in my pajamas at my kitchen table writing this book for you.

There's also a category of people beyond family and friend-ships that is important to touch on in this chapter. I call this category "everyone else you interact with during your brief stint on Earth." The two of us fall into this category, in the relation-ship of a writer sharing her thoughts and a reader digesting and considering them.

Although we have most likely never met, our brains have a relationship thanks to you picking up this book. The same type of relationship extends to everyone who we happen to pass in the street and make eye contact with and choose whether or not to smile at, the barista who makes our coffee, the flight attendant who serves our cross-country trip.

"Spread love everywhere you go. Let no one ever come to you without leaving happier." - Mother Teresa

These relationships, in my perspective, are important, because they're opportunities for spreading or sapping joy, for expanding or shrinking our webs, for growing or declining in our human potential. I don't believe that a neutral interaction exists. And it's hard to consistently show love and kindness, trust me I know. I regularly lose my patience on perfectly nice strangers.

One time, after an extremely long flight delay, I lost all perspective and actually accused a flight attendant of stealing my Kindle (long story…). I know, so awful. Ugh, I still feel terrible about that. And me being a big ol' brat probably infected that woman's mind with negativity, and, if she is anything like the rest of us, she probably spread it to other perfectly innocent passengers.

Our actions create a response in other people's minds, and also sometimes a physiological response. This is a fact; reread the chapter on mindset if you don't believe me. Negativity is viral and has the power to grow exponentially as we impact other people's minds and subsequent actions.

Imagine if I spent the whole time in this book talking about how brilliant and rich I was, how perfect my life and marriage were, how easy and delightful and amazing everything was all around me. You would probably (and justifiably so) hate me, and also finish this book feeling as though you are lacking, not smart enough, not attractive enough, and had chosen the wrong person in life. And you'd carry that negativity into other areas of your life, to your husband or your wife, to your kids, or colleagues. This book would have effectively stolen your joy and infected you with negativity that you would then unconsciously transfer to your entire web.

How to answer this question for yourself:

It is incredibly important to put some qualifications on who you invite into your life to absorb your time and energy, and allow those relationships that aren't quite working to fade away so you can fill the space with those that light you up. You're the only person who knows the kind of relationship that lights you up versus saps your joy, but there are some simple steps you can take to help you get started on improving the relationships you cultivate:

#1 Assess your own crab-status.

Be honest: are you a net positive person in the relationships you have? Are you normally positive, optimistic and supportive, or do you easily succumb to negativity, jealousy and fear? It's important that you start to take control of your own mind to become a net-positive person in order to cultivate better relationships. Read Chapter 4, "What about that big blob of cholesterol that tells me what to do" for how to do this yourself. Once you can firmly say you're (mostly) not a crab, proceed to step #2.

#2 Take stock of who you're spending time with.

Make a list of the people who you spend time with, including colleagues. Include people who you regularly interact with, either in person or virtually. Get 'em all down on paper.

#3 Consider who you're not spending time with, but want to be spending time with.

Add them to the above list.

#4 Evaluate these relationships based on what you need in your life.

It is my firm belief that there are really only three types of people in the world:

"Life-suckers," who sap joy and energy out of environments and people with their negativity and complaining and unproductive approach to life; "floaters," who are dependent on external circumstances and feel they have no control over anything; and "game-changers," who bring positivity and hope to everyone, even in the toughest times.

Take your list of people and allocate them to the above categories based on your experiences and feelings when you're with them and under their influence. Be ruthless, you'll destroy this paper later but it will help to clarify your thinking.

Then, consider how you allocate time to these relationships and where you might want to make some changes. What game-changers in your life should be receiving more of your time? What life-suckers should you be spending less time with? Where can you channel your net positive power on floaters to help lead them to become game changers?

(Obviously, this is not an exact science.)

#5 Eliminate or manage the relationships that aren't working to create more space for the ones you need.

My friend Erica and I were having dinner together in New York City over the summer, and she mentioned that she had a call with a friend she'd known forever and how draining it was, because the conversation was one-sided and negative and stressful, as it was every time they talked. Erica, by the way, is a person who exudes rainbows and sunshine—and that night, she was visibly dimmed, because she caught some of that negativity through her iPhone 6!

We talked about why she kept the relationship going despite how much it took from her, and she shared that, in a nutshell, she'd maintained the friendship out of habit and didn't want to hurt the other girl. She made the choice instead to let the other girl hurt her.

I think so many of us do this, and it's not doing anyone any favors. That night Erica and I reframed the conversation around treating other people the way we want to be treated ourselves. I said that I would be more hurt to discover someone remained my friend because they felt obligated to rather than having them fade away because it wasn't really working for them anymore.

Tibetan Buddhist teacher Chögyam Trungpa Rinpoche called this 'idiot compassion,' where you continue a friendship with someone not right for you because you cannot bear the discomfort of being truthful and upsetting the other person. He actually frames this as selfishness, because you put your own need for comfort over the other person's need for your honesty and authenticity.

Sometimes it's not as obvious when a relationship isn't right, but more of a sense that you're a better person when you're not around certain people who have the power to influence your behavior. I know amazing people who love to drink all day long on Saturdays and that is just not my style, because it's my one focused day to work out and take care of myself and my relationship with my husband. I'd rather skip the brunches and let the relationship fade than compromise what I value for myself.

Skipping all the boozy Saturday brunches allowed me to build a habit of going to the gym every Saturday morning and a years-long friendship with my personal trainer slash life coach whose constant pushing and questioning about this book helped me to write it!

#6 Create a relationship mantra.

As a reminder, Bronnie Ware taught us that two of the top five regrets of the dying are related to relationships. For me, it's helpful to have a mantra to orient me to what's important during the swirl of my daily life. Writing a mantra that reflects what you care about in your relationships and what you personally want to do in order to cultivate them can help you stay focused and build stronger connections with the people you love the most.

I'm sharing my mantra with you as an example and as inspiration as you write your own - this is adapted from what I learned in Matthew Kelly's book 'Perfectly Yourself':

My relationships are the best gift I've been given, and they are my biggest responsibility. The primary purpose of each of my relationships is to help each other become better versions of ourselves by sharing our authentic experiences, perspectives, and gifts. I will be open to new connections, because that is a source of growth in life—and I will seek and cultivate friendships that bring me to life, and distance myself from relationships that drain me and influence me to betray my values. I aspire to have the kind of quality relationships that inspire others in how they approach developing, growing, and cultivating this important area of their lives.

Summary of the key takeaway from this chapter:

Keep company only with people who uplift you (as much as practically possible), whose presence calls forth your best. Positivity and right thinking are as contagious as negativity and wrong thinking.

Recommended books with more research, ideas, and practical tips to answer this question:

Perfectly Yourself by Matthew Kelly
Stumbling on Happiness by Daniel Gilbert
Scary Close by Don Miller

CHAPTER 6

How do I pay for this?

An attitude on acquiring wealth

Other forms of this question include statements like, "Wealth redistribution is the solution for everything wrong with humanity" or, "My retirement plan is to marry well" or, "I justify purchases I cannot afford, because you can't take your money to the grave" or, "I could never afford that."

"Only when he has ceased to need things can a man truly be his own master and so really exist." - Anwar Sadat

A few years ago, James Altucher—an incredibly wealthy hedge fund manager and founder of more than twenty companies—was asked to share what keeps him up at night. He said he used to always worry that he was about to go broke. He shared that it was a symptom of his upbringing. His father was an entrepreneur who was always chasing the "next big thing" to make them rich, never achieved financial success, and eventually bankrupted the family. James went on to make a ton of money himself then lose it all, along with his marriage and house. It forced him to reflect on what worked and what didn't when it comes to accumulating money, and his insight was this:

"I think less about money and more about my health. For me the key to having a good relationship with money is to realize that money is much less important than I always thought it was. What's much more important is my belief in myself. I find that money is just a byproduct of living a healthy life. Am I constantly generating ideas and…exercising my idea muscle? And am I grateful for what I have? I started focusing everyday on improving my life physically, emotionally, mentally, and spiritually…by just 1%.

Instead of going out drinking and eating—and not exercising and not sleeping—I had to focus on my physical health. I had to focus on just being around people who I really enjoyed, and who trusted me and loved me. The best predictor of a successful tomorrow is to have a successful today. And the only way to have a successful today is to be healthy in those areas I just described. If every day I do those things, then…I will have money." - James Altucher

The "scarcity complex" is incredibly common in practically every human being wandering around this Earth in their meat suits, maybe even a survival instinct. It's also a mindset that has extremely negative ramifications on our life outcomes. Sendhil Mullainathan, a professor of economics at Harvard University and recipient of the MacArthur Foundation "genius grant," and Eldar Shafir, a psychology professor at Princeton University, wrote an entire book on this called "Scarcity" which covers how the scarcity complex shapes our thoughts, feeling, choices, and behaviors.

The key takeaway is that scarcity of money—either real or imagined—leads to diminished "bandwidth" (ability of the mind to hold information in the forefront of consciousness) and, therefore, "tunneling" (the intense focus on what is most immediate or important and the neglect of other issues). It creates a mindset that basically makes you dumber, resulting in flawed decisions concerning matters both related and unrelated to the scarce resource.

It's because this belief that there isn't enough of something makes people focus on the immediate pressures of what they believe they need, at the expense of long-range planning. For example, someone low on cash might take out a high-interest loan only to find themselves even worse later on. Or, a busy CEO might borrow time from a future project to get something done today, only to find herself strapped for time down the road.

Scarcity becomes a positive reinforcement cycle, where scarce thinking actually can create real scarcity. The authors refer to this self-defeating behavior as the "scarcity trap" where the poor get poorer and the busy get busier and both get dumber (or, have "reduced cognitive functioning in all matters").

The reason I loved James Altucher's response to how he addressed his own scarcity complex is because he talks about money as a byproduct of belief in himself, of his energy, and of the value he expends in how he generates and acts on ideas.

Although we focus so much on its physical, measurable, accumulate-able paper and digital forms, money, at the end of the day, is simply a construct and a belief system that was created around 600 B.C. to represent the value of goods and services, because the bartering system ceased to be practical in a growing economy.

It's not surprising that we have deep-seated emotions and beliefs about money as a scarce physical resource when you consider that it was carried around as coins or papers in the vulnerable, easy-to-pick pockets of our ancestors for roughly 2,500 years of human history until FDIC-insured banks came on the scene ninety years ago and credit cards popped up a decade later.

We're now shifting to a world of decentralized cryptocurrency and new forms of modern bartering, which would probably cause a mass meltdown of our relatives who clung to the gold standard and kept cash in their mattresses and drapes. *My dead great-grandmother, inventor of velvet curtains laced with Franklins, just rolled over in her grave.*

Despite the changing forms of money and long history we have of money being represented by an inherently physical substance that could be stolen, the underlying truth is that it is a representation of value for whatever is being exchanged. It is a belief that the tokens of the value we have delivered can continue to be exchanged for goods and services from other human beings.

Sorry, that got a little dense. Are you still with me?

My point is that focusing on "getting money" is not only ridiculous in this day and age, but also counterproductive, because it can only be generated by adding value to other human beings. It's an exchange of energy expended, as in you paid me $10 for this book because the energy it took for me to write these ideas for you to absorb in a single book was more valuable to you than the energy it took you to create that $10 you had to spend.

(And thanks, by the way, hope this book is thousands of times more valuable than that to you.)

As those very smart professors pointed out, if you focus on the outcome (currency) instead of on the value (energy) you're creating, your tunnel vision will prevent you from actually creating the value that generates the outcome you're looking for. Ultimately, you'll lock yourself into a very unfortunate positive reinforcement cycle and die really poor and sad and regretful—and in Bronnie Ware's book or something just like it.

Some of you might be thinking about the complexities of our financial system, corruption, systemic bias, socioeconomic advantages, etc., and I'm not denying those things are out there and of course play a part in the grand scheme of wealth accumulation. However, this book is focused on what we as individuals can control, and if you read the first few chapters, you'll remember that the only things we can control are our thoughts and actions in this exact moment and we're privileged in the way a literate person with at least $10 to spend is privileged.

So toppling capitalism will not be covered in this chapter. The key idea I want you to take away from this section is that you need to reframe how you think about money so that your focus is on adding value and not on getting currency. If you make other people's lives better, easier, or happier, money will follow. Let me say that a different way: deliver value, and you will get paid for results. The more value you deliver, the more you will be paid.

Sounds so simple, right? Just brainwash all your deep-seated beliefs and emotional baggage about money into value delivery and you'll be ultra-rich! End of chapter.

Just kidding, of course. There is a lot to unpack here, starting with how exactly we can address our own thoughts and actions as they relate to money and reframe our beliefs to center on the idea that money is simply a byproduct of effectively answering and acting on this question: How can I add more value to other people?

We covered the idea of adding value to other people as it relates to creating a fulfilling life in Chapter 2, "Why am I running around in this meat suit?" The Cliffs Notes version of that chapter, in case you didn't read it or need a refresher, is that:

Your purpose in life is to add value to other people in a way that makes their lives better, easier, or simpler. The most valuable assets that you have to give other people are your energy, enthusiasm, and joy. Your ability to produce and share those valuable assets is to figure out what gives you energy, enthusiasm, and joy and to create the capacity to do more of those things.

There's a whole exercise at the end of that chapter to help you figure out those things that give you joy. Presuming you've done that activity and have at least a sense of what gives you joy and where you want more capacity to do those life-giving things, this chapter will help you reframe your thinking and your beliefs around money in order to increase your capacity to add more value to other people through what you do while you're here on Earth.

You may have heard the term "abundance mindset" before, maybe from new-agey spiritual books or Deepak Chopra or your therapist or your Psychology 101 professor in college. It's the exact opposite of a scarcity mindset, and in being the exact opposite, it also has the opposite results in terms of creating money as a byproduct. As the famous quote suggests: "The secret to having it all is believing you already do." As the two very intelligent Ivy League professors and "Scarcity" authors noted, focusing on what you lack reduces your intelligence and ability to add value, because your attention is focused on resolving this real-or-imagined resource need for yourself.

The entire premise of this chapter is based on the inverse of that argument, that your intelligence and ability to add value is increased, because your attention is focused on all of the abundance you already enjoy, and it increases your capacity to add value to others and help them to resolve their needs.

Easier said than done, like all worthy ventures, so we'll get into the nuts and bolts of how to cure a scarcity complex, replace it with an abundance mindset, and add lots of value to other people with the byproduct of getting paid for it. We're going to start by looking at the practicality of your current money situation and getting all of that in order for those that might need it, then we'll dig in to your thoughts and beliefs around money in order to start shifting to a more abundant mindset. Finally, we'll cover some of the tangible things you can start doing immediately to add value to other people regardless of what you do or the level of joy it may currently be producing in your life.

My personal struggle with this question:

I'm going to keep this section short, and just tell you enough so that you don't feel like I'm preaching to you about money as a white girl born to a wealthy family who has never had a money concern in her life.

Because the truth is, I am a white girl born to a wealthy family who has never had a *real* money concern, but instead plenty of imagined ones and a lot of effed up beliefs and thinking about it. And I think it's important for you to know that, as I am sure that for many readers, our money situations are different. You may have had to overcome neglect and starvation as a child or get past incredibly dire circumstances through no fault of your own. Neither of us can control everything, particularly the circumstances of our own births and the challenges and setbacks we experienced in this world. I am going to ask you to humor my *imagined* money concerns as one person's example of the damaging consequences of a scarcity mindset and the benefits of refocusing on adding value to other people instead of fixing a money problem. If you still feel the need to send me hate mail, my email address is publicly available on my website, and my eighty-year-money-back-guarantee is still on the table.

OK, now that we've gotten the disclaimer out of the way, here's my short story on scarcity mindset that is going to make it seem like I blame my parents (sorry, Mom and Dad!), but I promise there will be an upswing at the end.

As mentioned previously, although it would be easier to write this if I grew up desperately poor in a rural Appalachian trailer or something, that is not my story. I grew up in a wealthy suburb of Chicago in a McMansion built not for impressiveness but simply to hold the volume that was my family—which amounted to five siblings, an epileptic yellow lab, and two of the most practical, pragmatic people you have ever met in your entire life. Those two people, my parents, spent a significant amount of energy trying to convince us that we were poor. My mom was the queen of feeding her family of eight on budget-friendly cream of mushroom soup-based casseroles, and my dad literally still wears things that he bought in the 1970s despite all of our collective efforts to hide and burn them.

The two of them were seemingly oblivious to the trappings of wealthy suburban living. For example, rather than hire a lawn service to take care of the house and *actual acre* of backyard, they woke us all up at the crack of 9 a.m. on Saturdays to do yard work—whether or not there was yard work to do. (I recall once participating in a "levelling the yard" exercise involving shoveling of loose dirt from the driveway to various sections of the lawn, and then replanting grass, which was futile save for satisfying my father's perfectionist need for a level lawn cultivated by a bunch of gangly, otherwise-useless kids.) I think it goes without saying that allowances were not doled out in my parent's home.

Anyway, my point in telling you all of this is because I believe that my upbringing gave me a scarcity complex. Although it gave me a great work ethic and taught me to think for myself, I essentially learned no money management skills and focused almost all of my energy on making money so that I could buy whatever I wanted and never again have to listen to Paul Kelly's perspectives on practical purchases. (Good alliteration there, yes? Might make this the sequel to this book, stay tuned...)

Most of my scarcity complex was driven by shame and feeling less-than, growing up with extremely wealthy friends who had generous allowances and Range Rovers—I couldn't keep up with some of the same interests and hobbies, because my family quite simply couldn't or wouldn't cover it.

I focused on what I didn't have but wanted, and started working the moment that I was legally allowed: folding sweaters at a local boutique, working behind the counter at a local bakery, lifeguarding at the local pool, waitressing, bartending and taking orders, cleaning the grill hood at a sports bar in college, and babysitting for extra cash whenever I could. I also started an eBay side hustle selling my old stuff.

The moment I got a *real* job paying a salary and benefits, my utter lack of money management skills kicked in full force. I immediately threw myself into living it up, treating myself to expensive clothes and meals and trips, overspending my credit card, making minimum payments on my college student loans, ignoring my savings account and 401k entirely, and, in general, totally screwing myself over. When I thought about saving money, my mind would wander to an image of me sitting forlorn on an old futon in a windowless room, eating lukewarm ramen noodles out of a Styrofoam cup.

When I thought about making money, I imagined scenes from "The Wolf of Wall Street" and felt a sense of shame that my inability to decipher the NASDAQ ticker was somewhat reminiscent of my inability to decipher my 6th grade French textbook. I also loved that Carrie Bradshaw quote about how she liked to see her money hanging in her closet. (WTF, Carrie?! So irresponsible! I know what NYC costs and your lifestyle does not add up! You should be in a lofted bunk bed in a broom closet on the Lower East Side with at least three roommates!) My point is, I had an extremely negative relationship with money that was focused on how to get more of it, so I could address what was lacking in my life. Textbook scarcity!

Thankfully, I had a wakeup call when I opened a TJ Maxx credit card and learned the hard way that they charged 20 percent interest or something like that. (WTF, TJ Maxx?!) It taught me an expensive but very valuable lesson and inspired me to ratchet back big-time. It didn't, however, resolve my scarcity complex. The extent of my personal finance strategy became to simply make sure I was living within my means, paying my bills on time, saving a little every month, and then buying whatever I wanted under those constraints while focusing on how I needed to make more money, in general, but not really sure how to go about it.

Although I wish I could tell you that there was some sort of epiphany (beyond that thing about being in debt to TJ Maxx, which really leads to some soul searching if I am being honest) that totally resolved my thinking, but there were really three things that happened that helped me:

#1 I married a CPA who was literally shell-shocked by my utter carelessness with money.

"How can you make so much and have saved so little!?" were his exact words when we had that talk that I think all people embarking on combining their lives and, potentially, bank accounts have. It was embarrassing, because I knew that he was right. He paid off my student loans, not me. He maxed out my 401k, not me. He took over managing our finances and investments, not me.

Then, gaining confidence in his plan to take full control of our financial future, he attempted to put me on a budget. We fought like Scotsmen, as they say—if one Scotsman were to have extremely irrational savings targets and thought dining at the Costco café for a $1.50 hot dog counted as "going out to lunch," while the other Scotsman were to give zero effs about these things and indulge her newlywed nesting instincts by buying expensive home accessories she did not need at Crate and Barrel.

Very long story short, I realized that we both needed to change (me more so, but the level of inner frugality he unleashed on me after three years of hiding it while dating was terrifying), and we fumbled around with different strategies that we never fully bought into. Then I discovered Ramit Sethi's book entitled "I Will Teach You To Be Rich," which is sort of a "get rich slow" scheme with the most pragmatic perspective on how to think about and manage money I've ever heard. It helped Wes and I to agree that we both wanted a comfortable life and to accumulate savings and wealth that would set us up for long-term success.

Once we were both on the same page, the conversation became about how to create a personal finance strategy that would enable our lifestyle and each of our individual priorities. It helped us to make small adjustments and do more thoughtful planning and spend more on what we actually cared about, because we took the time to establish the right foundation for ourselves. (I included his basic steps we used in the "How to answer this question for yourself" below.) Anyway, my point is that my critical first step was dealing with the practicalities of my current financial situation.

#2 I learned to appreciate what I had.

I wish there was a more dramatic and life-changing way to say that, because people used to tell me that and it had the net effect of an inspirational cat poster or notebooks with covers that say "Live, Laugh, Love." Side note: please stop producing these cliché wastes of paper, and I think you've created a market for me to make millions on demotivational cat posters and notebooks with covers that say "Die, Cry, Hate." Honestly, I hit the point where I hated my job and stumbled across this quote:

"The price of anything is the amount of life you exchange for it." - Henry David Thoreau

It inspired me to deeply consider how much life I'd exchanged to date for the things I owned, and I started to feel owned by my things. The thought of quitting my high-paying job to do something more creative made me reflect on how I would handle cutting back my spending, and I started evaluating everything, especially what was motivating my desire to consume. It helped me to learn what I truly value, what's worth spending on versus what's not, and to also appreciate all of the abundance I had in my life. Training myself to overcome my urges to consume and to use what I had helped me to build my gratitude muscle and refocus on what really mattered to me and what I actually valued.

#3 I realized that adding value was the real secret.

My income has grown with my ability to add value, and there is no other way around it. I'm not going to elaborate on this point: your ability to make another person's life easier, simpler, or happier will always translate into rewards, including additional responsibilities, promotions, salary increases, bonuses, and people willing to pay you for the service or product that's helping so many others. There is no other way, and there's nothing more to say about it.

How to answer this question for yourself:

#1 Deal with the practicalities of your current money situation and get your finances in order.

Stare your financials in the face. Gather the facts on your current financial position. This includes debts, expenses, savings, what you have coming in, and where you're spending your disposable income. This is your current financial position.

Figure out your non-negotiable expenses: If you want to improve your financial position, you need to consider what expenses are most important to you, be it a beautiful apartment in a desirable location, designer bags, or traveling the world. When I sat down to really think long and hard about my non-negotiables, it was a surprisingly short list.

If you have debt to pay off or need to be saving more, scale back on "negotiable expenses": Cut back on every possible expense that does not support your top priority or priorities. For me, that meant cutting out things like coffee shops, frequent fancy dinners, manicures/pedicures, and Sephora runs, which sometimes ended up costing hundreds of dollars in the course of a month. And that outrageous cable package for my husband…Netflix it is, folks!

Pay off your debts. This should go without saying, but paying off any debt should be priority number one. There's a lot out there on debt payment strategy, but fundamentally you want to get rid of it as quickly as possible.

Decide your goals. This should be how much you want to save, invest, put into retirement accounts, etc. There are a lot of opinions on how much you need to save, how much you need to retire, but I find it overwhelming and like the advice to figure out what three months of your nonnegotiable expenses are and to have a minimum of that amount in liquid cash savings, and then just build from there.

If you understand investments, go for it. If you don't, educate yourself or just hunker down on what you do understand that appreciates in value. At a minimum, max out your 401k if you have one. Sadly, I hadn't been doing this and have lost a lot of free money. If you've got a corporate 401k, figure out what your company will match, and max out that percentage. Then sit on it and watch the dollars roll in. Your 80-year-old self will thank you (in addition to judging your 25-year-old self for wasting what could have been 401k match dollars on TJ Maxx shoes). Live and learn.

Get a system in place. Make it an extremely simple document so you can manage it over time. Put all of your financial accounts (banking, credit cards, loans, and investments), login/passwords, interest percentages, monthly contributions, and other details into one place so you've got the ability to check in and keep your system working seamlessly. And, obviously, store it in a safe place.

Sit back and watch the dollaz roll in! Just kidding, this passive personal finance system is definitely not the end of the chapter on money. The whole point of this first step in how to answer the question "What do I do about money?" is to simply get the practicalities in order and set up a reliable structure that enables savings to become automatic, and also focuses your disposable income on what you actually care about. I really love Ramit's tip for having separate, labeled "accounts" to save for the things on your non-negotiable list. Imagine how much more free you'd feel traveling knowing that you've earmarked and already have saved the thousands it's going to cost! As you increase your income over time (which we'll cover on the next couple of tips), this system can also flex to accommodate additional accounts and investments.

#2 Get extremely grateful for what you already have.

Look back at everything you've been given, all the blessings in your life up until this exact point in your life, and list them out in very specific detail. For me, my list starts with being born into a healthy, capable meat suit in a country that values life, education, and human potential, to parents who loved me unconditionally, who sacrificed nights of sleep and their own interests and a lengthy tab of expenses required to raise me and put me through high school and college, in an environment where I could make wonderful friends who challenged me and opened my world.

Even the hardships we experience in life come with silver linings and should make it on your list. For me, having a drug addict in my family made me into a person who is obsessed with unmet potential, and it's helped me to focus on growing myself and helping others see where they can also do, and be, more of themselves in this world. It's amazing what happens to your mind when you take the time to do this. The first time I did it, I cried and literally felt like there was nothing in the world that I should ever complain about.

Create this list for yourself, and save it in a safe place for when you need to revisit it. I revisit mine when I start to get into those weird moods where I feel like everything is falling apart, and my higher voice chimes in, usually with a swift, blunt, "Get it together, Colleen! You have everything!"

Get in the habit of adding to this list of what you're grateful for every single morning. Buy a small notebook and keep it in a place where you find yourself seated with time to think in the morning, maybe by your bedside or in the drawer where you keep the coffee filters. Mine is next to my couch, where I like to light the fire and think for an hour before starting my day. Focus on the small things that you appreciate in your daily life that so often get overlooked by the negatives. Every morning while having your coffee, write "5 Things I am Grateful for Today" and simply list them out with no judgment for how miniscule they may be (for example, having a moment to drink your coffee alone might be one).

#3 Outline what you need to have an "ideal day" going forward from this point in life to reframe your needs.

On a sheet of paper, make seven sections, one for each day of the week, Monday through Sunday.

Go through each day's section and think about the last time you had a really great day on that particular day of the week. Write down the specifics of what made that day great—it can be as miniscule or significant as you want. For example, my Sunday has "Went to 8am Bikram yoga" and "Read the Sunday paper over coffee with Wes" and "Had a leisurely meal with family," and my Monday has "Woke up an hour before I needed to start getting ready to spend time alone to reflect and write," and "Outlined my key priorities for the work week" and "Connected with colleagues outside of work."

Go back to each day and identify what things you wrote down that can be repeated every single week, and highlight them. These are your actual needs, the elements of your day-to-day life that are worth exchanging something to recreate over and over again to keep you in an abundance mindset. For me, hiring help with cleaning my house is a cost that is well worth it, because it allows me time on Fridays to connect with colleagues after work instead of running home to clean. Or, saying no to a meeting request early on a Monday morning is a risk-cost I am willing to take, because it allows me time to start my week with the right mindset and, therefore, increase my capacity to add value.

#4 Teach yourself to add as much value to other people as possible, looking above and beyond the physical product or service you deliver that generates the dollars (or Euros or whatever currency you use).

Consider how you can make other people's lives easier, simpler or happier - and in a way that gives you joy, energy and increases your capacity. Think about where there are problems that need to be solved, and how you can help to be part of the solution. Manage your money mindset, and stamp out thoughts of fear and scarcity as they arise by channeling gratitude for all of the blessings you enjoy in life.

Summary of the key takeaway from this chapter:

Get your act together and stop being irresponsible and allowing a negative relationship with money to fester in your life. Cure your scarcity complex by focusing all of your attention on gratitude for what you already have, and you'll increase your capacity to add value to other people—and wealth will follow you everywhere.

Recommended books with more research, ideas, and practical tips to answer this question:

Tap Dancing to Work by Warren Buffet
I Will Teach You to be Rich by Ramit Sethi
The Law of Divine Compensation by Marianne Williamson
You are a Badass at Making Money by Jen Sincero

CHAPTER 7

When do I need to have this all figured out?

A beginner's position on how to let go of
your white-knuckle grip on life

Other forms of this question include thoughts, such as, "At one point in my life, I wanted to be a veterinarian, because I believe you can see God in the innocent eyes of animals. But animals and God pay beans, so I chose a more secure future selling life insurance. It's fine, I'm fine. I can afford my mortgage, and I have a cat at home so it all worked out." Or, "All I want is to control every variable in my entire life and be 100 percent sure that everything will work out for me. Is that too much to ask?"

"As your faith is strengthened, you will find that there is no longer a need to have a sense of control, that things will flow as they will, and that you will flow with them, to your great delight and benefit." - Wingate Paine

One of my mentees, a young consultant with just two years of post-college experience, called me last week to talk about her concern that she didn't have everything figured out. "I just feel like I should have made more progress by now and have a better idea of the direction I want to go." It struck me as both ridiculous and familiar.

It was ridiculous because I cannot think of one person who would ever be interested in meeting or hiring a 24-year-old who has it all figured out. What I wanted to say was, "If I know nothing, you definitely know nothing, so calm the eff down!" What I actually said was something about how we tend to crave a neatly paved path, one that will lead us to proven success, and we expect it to feel right and to get some sort of external validation or pat on the back that we've made the right choices and are doing a great job. Especially coming out of college and fresh off our predictable, sequential, milestone, and grade-driven life. By the way, that external validation and pat on the back are never coming.

"You have to be comfortable not knowing exactly where life is going. That's how I've learned to keep anxiety away. All we can do is learn how to make the best decisions that are in front of us, and trust that, over time, the odds will be in our favor." - Annie Duke, world champion poker player

It was familiar, also, because I'd gone through the same struggle, feeling like I should have done more or made more progress or met a certain life milestone. I compared myself to other people, using their lives as a benchmark of my own success and always feeling like I was behind, making bad choices, or going the wrong way.

The reality is that we are not supposed to have it all figured out. How utterly boring would that be if we could neatly plot out exactly what our lives would look like? There are books on this. I am pretty sure that's the whole point of Lois Lowry's "The Giver," which I personally found to be deeply depressing/ terrifying and think I still would have felt that way even in the depths of my cravings to have full control of both the steering wheel and the road design of my life. It is my firm belief that one of the greatest lies of our time is that other people have it all figured out, and we're alone flailing out here in the wind with our flaws and our complete lack of assurance that we're doing anything right.

"Many times the wrong train took me to the right place."
- Paulo Coelho

That was just a long-winded way of saying that we are sup- posed to struggle, to figure out how be true to what makes us unique, to seize opportunities as they arise, to seek growth and challenge, forge our own path, and have faith that it will lead us in the direction our future selves will want to be. What I do not know is how much of this naturally unfolds as we mature, versus how much requires active effort to develop self-awareness and push ourselves to grow. As an ultra-uncool person who tries really hard at everything, I'm gonna go with the latter.

"Intelligence is the ability to adapt to change." - Stephen Hawking

Romantic poet John Keats (who happens to be one of the most influential, creative geniuses humanity has produced) coined the term "negative capability" that we're exploring in this chapter. It's the willingness to embrace uncertainty, live with mystery, and make peace with ambiguity, and rest in the fact that that life is about living the questions themselves. A white-knuckle grip on life cannot coexist with negative capability.

So many of us do not have the ability to embrace uncer- tainty, to live with the questions, to address what Robert Frost famously called "the big fat lump in your throat," the home-sickness, the heartbreak, the aching void, or vague sense that something is missing. Basically, that there is more to life than what it is we're doing.

We crave control, allowing our white-knuckle grip on our lives to steer us during those critical pivot points, where we teeter between the safe and uncertain, the well-worn path, and the one that requires us to bring our own machete and figure out how to use a compass. We rationalize and quietly talk ourselves out of what we feel compelled to do, choosing practical and reasonable and proven paths, because it makes us feel as though we have safeguarded our futures. We seek to be sensible, careful, and tell ourselves that we are striking a compromise, that we're selecting a path that allows us to be self-sufficient.

We convince ourselves that the pull we feel towards what brings us joy is impractical, that it cannot make us a living, that we're not smart enough or pretty enough or talented enough to make it happen. We begin to believe our own self-doubt, resisting that pull towards what lights us up until it becomes a dull ache that becomes easy to ignore over time as long as we're not alone with our thoughts for too long. We tell ourselves that one day something will change, but for now it's better to be safe. And we're not profoundly unhappy, but deep inside, we know that we settled and wonder what life might be like had we chosen an alternate path during those moments where we teetered away from the uncertain.

The paradox in all of this is that our self-induced attempt to failure-proof ourselves by controlling all the variables is what limits our imagination and possibilities and causes us to fail to reach our potential. We settle in exchange for security, but the dangerous thing—now more than ever before—is that security does not exist in our ever-evolving, consistently disrupted world.

My personal struggle with this question:

At heart, I am an artist and a writer, and I have always known this about myself. I started college as an art history major but switched to print-editorial journalism, because I felt like I wasn't being fully tapped. There was a moment towards the end of college when something switched in my mind—like the reality of looming adulthood settling in—where I made a choice to seek a comfortable and predictable corporate path, telling myself I could always become an artist or a writer later in life. But I thought following my heart couldn't make me money, that it wouldn't be enjoyable if I did it full time, and that I needed "real world experience," whatever that meant.

So I started an economically secure 9-5 job in a beige cubicle doing pricing and margin analysis, bid reviews, and customer segmentation for a line of frozen baked goods. Once I learned what COGS (cost of goods sold) and PNLS (profit and loss statements) were, I was actually pretty good at it, but deep inside I was miserable. I told myself that I was a business management associate, not a creative person. I worked in a large, buzzing corporate complex with an onsite hairdresser and all-you-can-drink coffee and made sure the products we sold to Walmart sat high enough in their clamshells to be appealing to customers and could last a few days on the shelf to generate repeat buyers.

The company transferred me to D.C. to work in a field role calling on contracted accounts that were supposed to meet certain volume targets and were missing the mark, and the best part about it was that I got my first *real* apartment that I decorated with the kind of zeal Martha Stewart must have had upon exiting prison. The second best part was using the sleuthing skills I learned in my journalism classes to leave cryptic messages in the voicemail boxes of buyers across the DMV area that I would visit "Monday by 9 am" unless they called me back to tell me not to come. It was like a contest with myself to see if I would get kicked out of a building. Other than that, it was soul-crushing. Luckily, I met my husband Wes, who was enough of a reason to quit when they tried to transfer me again.

I ended up with another economically secure job in management consulting, which I promptly detested and used my handy-dandy cold calling skills to line up meetings with editors of online publications I wanted to write for, kicked off a freelance writing side hustle, and started my own blog. But I basically shared my blog with no one, because I was afraid of being judged as I produced mediocre posts about myriad topics that I didn't really care about. But it felt safe, because it appeared that is what other people did. Also, I didn't want the corporate folk to find it and judge me for all the selfies. So, basically, I hovered on the sidelines and created stuff in a very small, safe way and continued to go full speed ahead on my management consulting career, because it was respectable and practical and lucrative.

I remember getting promoted at work and then having this moment of deep anxiety about the tensions I'd created in my own life between my intentionally separate corporate and creative ventures. Once I woke up in the middle of the night in a cold sweat, mind racing with thoughts of my executive clients Googling me, finding my half-baked blog that I coded myself, telling the partners about my ridiculously indulgent display on the Internet, and watching me get fired in a dramatic scene where I was called an embarrassment to the firm. "You need to quit writing," I told myself. "You're getting too old for this, it's stupid, you're not talented enough to take it anywhere, and you don't even know what you want to write about." I went to bed convinced that I would delete my blog, quit freelancing, and hunker down on the safe, failure-proof career I'd chosen for myself.

But my bossy inner voice, that I'd spent a lot of time tuning in to by this point in my life, wouldn't shut the eff up about it. She actually yelled at me to not be such a weak, boring scared-y cat and said things like, "Is this what you'd advise your future daughter to do? To let imagined judgment from random people stop her from doing things that light her up? STAAAAP." So I couldn't do it, instead deciding it was time to stop playing down what I loved and start taking my creative writing as seriously as I'd been taking my corporate path. It was a conscious decision to let go of fear entirely and to start looking at the opportunity to layer my creative passions into my life in a much bigger way.

Strangely, when I let go of all of this fear, both my corporate and creative efforts lit up in a whole new way. I discovered channels to bring the topics I loved to read and think and write about to my full-time job, found forums to speak about what I was learning, and recognized a new path of convergence that my black-and-white, fearful mindset of limited possibilities hadn't seen before—but likely had been there all along.

If I am being honest, I am still in the midst of my process of letting go of my own white-knuckle grip on life and being authentic about what I truly love to do that brings me joy. I certainly don't have all of the answers, and writing this book has been a very big step in my path to respond to what I feel called to do in my life. At this point, I am operating almost fully in the gray space, the unknown, the uncertainty, the mystery of life that is guided only by the confidence I have developed through understanding my inherent value enough to stop worrying about being judged and better defining the purpose of why I am here. It's a wonderful place to be, not immune to anxiety or self-doubt but much more resilient and trusting and assured than I ever felt possible for myself.

How to answer this question for yourself:

Our ability to operate in Keats'"negative capability," where we can imagine and create, innovate, adapt, and explore the unknown and thrive in the mysteries of this life, is not only a capability that helps you live out what brings you joy but is also a uniquely human advantage in our quickly shifting labor market.

Whether you're just starting out or reimagining at a halfway point, now is the time to surrender control, to let go of your need for a predictable path, to throw caution to the wind, and to release the chokehold you've had on your inner voice asking for more. Acknowledge that the world is changing more rapidly than ever before. There isn't a best course of action, a right way to go. Instead, listen to your inner voice, have a vision for your life, muster the courage to get over your own fears and get started doing what you love. Don't place limits on the possibilities of where it can go, don't make compromises, and don't waste any more time. Start immediately. Today. Now.

If you're not sure where to start, remember that's normal. It's your negative capability begging to be developed. Don't let your fear squash it. Be brave. Here's an activity to get you started:

#1 Evaluate where you are today in the most important areas of your life.

Or said more simply, assess your ability to answer each of the questions posed in the chapter titles of this book. Do all of the exercises provided and think through where you have the most room for growth. Give yourself credit for the answers that come easily to you, and focus on the places where the answers have not revealed themselves quite yet.

#2 Do "fear-setting" for the areas of your life where you still have room to grow.

Fear-setting, according to author and lifestyle guru Tim Fer-riss, is an exercise that is intended to help you get over whatever is causing you to feel like you need to control everything. It's pretty simple: just outline the scenarios that are causing you to be afraid, thinking of the worst possible outcome in each of those situations. Consider what you'd do if you found yourself in the worst-case scenario and what you'd do to overcome it.

In my life, I have fears on "Why am I running around in this meat suit?" because, although I know my purpose is related to sharing my creative talents, I don't yet have empirical proof of that. My worst case scenario fears are that this book I am writing sells two copies and everyone hates it, that my safe and very comfortable day job that pays my bills rejects me, and that I one day discover my purpose is to be a politician but it's simply not possible to distance myself from all of the selfies-with-deep-thoughts posts I've published to the World Wide Web. Maybe these things sound silly to you, but they were real fears of mine that held me back from doing what I needed to do in order to answer that question myself. Once I realized that, in each worst case scenario, I'd be totally fine and had a rough plan for what I'd do, it made it so much easier to make progress.

#3 Define who (not what) you want to be in 5 years.

This is an activity I did in my mid-twenties amidst the full-fledged quarter-life crisis referenced in previous chapters. (Special shoutout to my personal hero, Dr. Meg Jay, for helping me through this trying time.) After I read "The Defining Decade" and completed my "purpose filter" exercise, I wrote out in explicit detail who I wanted to be by the time I was thirty-two. So much seemingly ridiculous detail was spent on that vision, including things like "get paid to fly first class and stay in fancy hotels," and "work with brilliant people who will make me smarter," and "wear really fancy suits and be a strong role model that helps to bring up others in their careers." When I look back at that vision, it's uncanny how much of it has manifested in my life today. Having a vision is also incredibly comforting and helped me to let go of some of the angst I had, because I started to see more clearly what I wanted and how to get there.

#4 Work backwards from there, identifying the major goals and milestones you need to make your life-in-five-years possible.

This is as simple as it sounds. You can't have it all planned out, but you can put out some major things that will get you there in terms of what is well within your reach. My goals included taking on experiences that scared me and pushed me out of my comfort zone, of writing and putting my work out into the world without fearing how it would be received, and making genuine friends at work across levels to help me bring more of my authentic self to the table.

#5 Simplify your life to eliminate the small details that distract you.

These little things do not matter in the big picture of life. Honestly, I could write an entire chapter on this. If you're worried about not having enough time, cut out all of the non-value-added stuff that sucks it—the activities, people, things that drain your energy and sap your joy. Get rid of stuff, outsource wherever possible, and get to a model in your day-to-day life that supports your needs and move forward from there.

We so easily get distracted by things like, "You know what I want? A brand new house!" and suddenly a million dollar mortgage disincentivizes us from pushing ourselves to take the risks to move closer to our purpose. Figure out what's distracting you, and do everything in your power to minimize or eliminate those activities, people, and things.

#6 Do something to move yourself forward every day.

Small, daily thoughts and actions amount to incredible compound returns. Figure out the one-hundred-dollar things and the one-dollar things that you do every day, the activities that are most important, that drive the most value, and progress towards your vision versus the ones that are essentially low-priority. Consciously figure out the one-hundred-dollar things you need to do every day, and prioritize everything around those things. Plan to do them when you have the most energy and motivation. For me, that time is really early in the a.m. when I'm having my coffee and just starting my day.

#7 Relax your white-knuckle grip and give it time.

We talked about the scarcity complex in terms of money, but it's a thing for how we manage and relate to time, too. In fact, in some ways it's a paradox, because time is our most precious resource. But worrying about running out of time is exactly how we waste it! I have many friends who have shared with me their fears of "running out of time" to get married, to have a baby, to have accomplished a certain milestone, to prevent wrinkles, etc.

My dad is doing this too, freaking out about end-of-life ailments and whether he has enough time to reverse the aging process. It's understandable why we do this, because we get so many cultural cues about the cadence of life that we believe we're supposed to follow. But it's a lie and a joy-killer. Don't put a ceiling on when certain milestones must be met, on when you must achieve something, on how long you can live. If you understand your vision and the most important things to be doing each day that you're here, you can enjoy the moment and trust that the rest of it will unfold the way it's supposed to for you.

Summary of the key takeaway from this chapter:

As hard as you may have tried to date, it's impossible to control the mysterious and uncertain nature of this life, to predict all the variables, to protect yourself from failure and pain and surprise. Recognize that the only thing you can control are your own thoughts and actions, and you literally have all the time in the world. So calm the eff down and focus on this exact moment, resting in the vision you have for where you want this moment, and all of the others after it, to lead.

Recommended books with more research, ideas, and practical tips to answer this question:

Surely You Must be Joking Mr. Feynman by Richard Feynman
The Big Leap by Gay Hendricks
The Subtle Art of Not Giving a F*ck by Mark Manson
Life is What You Make It by Warren Buffet

Conclusion

"Destiny is not a matter of chance, but a choice. Not something to wish for, but to attain." - William Jennings Bryan

It seems like a book should be concluded with a little bit on why it was written in the first place. Which, to be honest, is one of the hardest questions for a writer to answer. I assume this, because it was hard for me to answer myself, and I've clearly established a pattern of projecting my anecdotal experiences onto basically everyone.

When I thought about why I wrote this, I considered being blatantly honest: "Um, I had this little inner pull for years to write a book but I didn't really know what it was going to be about until I started the bizarre and cyclical process of writing vigorously, wallowing in self-doubt, deleting everything, and starting over. And here we are!" or "Honestly, I dumped the 736 half-full, embarrassingly disorganized notebooks of ideas, magazine clippings, quotes, coffee stains and postcards stuffed in baskets across my home onto my kitchen table and realized there were some themes behind what I was paying attention to all along, so I got wine drunk and wrote it all down into an outline that turned out to be really great."

These are true, but not complete answers.

The reality is, after parsing out the creative process stuff and ego stuff, I realized there are things I need to share related to what I've learned about "the human condition" (fancy way of saying, "the effing crazy swirl that it is to be alive"). I felt pulled to put all of myself into this book, to use what I have experienced and learned to infect other people with the sense of possibility I've imagined for my life that kept me going through the darkest times, to share the tools I discovered and used to create the fulfilling life of my dreams.

Put more eloquently, I believe we're taught to think in exceptionally stale ways about ourselves and our potential in life. As Barry Schwartz describes it, we're overwhelmed with external influences, and lack a philosophy or mental framework for filtering options and making intentional decisions based on who we are and what we value. This is a problem for us as individuals, but even more so for our world, which desperately needs people to change their thinking, live up to their highest potential, and fix all our effing problems.

Ok, now that the "why I wrote this" is out of the way, let's shift the focus back on over to you. Because it is not lost on me that this short book is dense on ideas and suggestions, and the absolute last thing I would want any reader of this book to feel is overwhelmed and not sure where to start.

So! Let's close this thing on that very topic: what you should do now, assuming you've found some ideas that resonate and are worth trying in your own life, and completed the exercises suggested in those chapters to help structure and clarify your thinking to better define the outcomes you want. Because defining what you actually want is only half of the challenge.

The other half of the challenge is doing the necessary work to bring what you want out of your life to fruition. We have a lot of strange ideas and assumptions about success, that it's an instantaneous thing: you meet the love of your life, the dream opportunity lands on your lap, you find the right diet pill and your hot body is available to you a week later, and so on. The reality is that successful life outcomes, however we define them, are built upon tiny, daily thoughts and actions. Those tiny, daily thoughts and actions must change if you want your life outcomes to change, and they must change in a way that aligns to the realities you would like to produce in your own life.

"Action expresses priorities." -Gandhi

It took me years of pain, mistakes and reflection to learn this — and I believe all of it could have been avoided if I knew what to ask myself about the most important areas of my life to define what I wanted, and took the time to build the daily habit of channeling my thinking in order to produce those outcomes. It wasn't until I started the daily practice that I'm going to tell you about in the following paragraphs that my life started to dramatically change for the better.

This daily practice is small and very tactical, something you'll do every morning over your coffee at your kitchen table, or at your desk, or on the train, or wherever you can find 10 minutes of solitude to think.

The first step is to channel your mind towards gratitude and abundance, by identifying five things in your life — right now — that you appreciate. Because as we learned in the chapter on wealth, failing to cultivate an abundance mindset and appreciating all the blessings you enjoy will keep you poor and sad. No reader of mine shall live this way!

The second step is to list out at least one goal — as if it has already happened — for each of the most important life topics we covered in this book — for a total of 10 goals. For me, the relationship topic is a big one right now, and one of my goals is, "Wes and I have the most amazing and life-giving marriage, and it inspires others to invest in their own."

The reason you must write each of your goals as if it has already happened is because that will force your thoughts to align to that reality. There are some psychological facts about how powerful this is but instead of boring you with that, just trust me and do it because it's low risk and I am running low on patience to finish this chapter. Mmkay? Great.

The third step is to choose one action — just one — that you can do that very day to help you get closer to your goals. For me, it's sometimes as simple as sending an email or text to my husband to tell him something I appreciate about him. Other times it's planning a date I know we will both enjoy, or clearing all plans for a Sunday so we can just rest and enjoy each other's company with no pressures of errands and appointments and to-do's. Choose just one thing, and make sure it's something you can realistically accomplish that very day.

All you need is a notebook and a pen, and simply write out the questions above. For those who prefer a bit more structure, visit my website colleenbordeaux.com/book, where I have (hopefully by the time you're reading this) created a journal or something that makes it easier for you while also earning incremental revenue for me because that's what professionals do, folks. That's what they do. And I am a professional! At the very minimum, I'll have it as a free download template.

Anyway, if you define your own answers to the questions we covered in this short book, and do this process every day, I guarantee you will get the highest possible return on each day of your very short life.

Also, I have a few reminders for you before we part ways. First, no one on Earth has it all figured out, and that's the amazing and terrifying thing about life. We're each works in progress, constantly morphing and growing. So many people end up regretting their lives because they simply lack vision and clarity for where they want all of that change to lead them. Those who live fulfilling lives that leave the world a better place began with the end in mind, channeled the older, wiser versions of themselves and asked what they really, really wanted in the most important areas of their lives.

As you read this sentence, 80-year-old-you is staring right at you through a bizarre space-age contraption that cuts through space and time (but is governed by laws that prevent it from interfering with the present as it unfolds), and is seriously so happy that you're finally defining what you really, really want, right now, regardless of what's expected of you.

The answer to the original question, "Am I doing this right?" is this: if you're still asking yourself that question, the answer is no. Keep working on your answers to the key questions about the most important areas of your life, and you'll get there.

Last but not least, for everyone who feels this is an off-the-cuff way of discussing life's most important questions, my 80-year-old self told me that discussing things in on-the-cuff ways is boring and pointless.

This feels like a good spot to end this, right? I think so, too.

Ok, bye. Good luck, see you in Tuscany.

GRATITUDE, BECAUSE BOOKS AREN'T WRITTEN ALONE

Acknowl-edgements

If you read this entire book, you'll remember the part on relationships, and how important it is to do everything in your power to have as many game-changers in your web as humanly possible. I am fortunate to have the most incredible and diverse set of game-changers in my life, each of whom made this book possible.

First, my family: Wes, who literally has been my rock and mirror, the person who has made me into the human being I am today, who balances my weaknesses through his set of perfectly matched strengths, who supported and shared my writing even when it was fashion fluff that his friends made fun of. My mom, whose love, kindness, generosity and willingness to be my sole reader when I first started blogging gave me the boosts I needed to keep going many times over. My dad, who taught me to think, to buck convention, to treat everyone the same, and first suggested I learn to control my own thoughts when I was in college and I wish I'd had enough wisdom to listen back then because I'd be president by now.

My siblings, each of whom supports my creative ventures in their own way, and help me see the world through their eyes so I can understand it and all the humans that live in it a little better.

Next, my friends: Michelle Roberts Smith, for her strong sense of self and ability to see the potential in all of her friends, for encouraging even my most ridiculous ideas and helping me hone the confidence to follow where they may lead. Jen Boulos Woodring, for being a force for positivity and good in my life since we were 4 years old, for encouraging me to stay true to myself and what makes me unique, for being a listening ear and open heart to me and everyone in her life. Ashley Zygmunt Gootee, for being a creative inspiration, for helping me hone confidence in my own style and voice, for being with my during the darkest and very best times since we were 15 years old.

Elise Rose Meyer, for being a source of both encouragement and pragmatism in my life, for showing what it looks like to be yourself regardless of the situation, for making it hip to be a square, for her intellect and appreciation of a healthy debate. Gill Casten, for being an effing weirdo with the strongest sense of self I've ever encountered, who inspires me to be more of myself, more real, and more present in life.

Jessie Wind Gregor, for starting a club called "I'm the sh*t" and inviting me to be the first and only member when we were awkward freshmen in college, two joyful souls who found each other laughing at our own jokes to of an audience of crickets in a depressing women's dorm. Jessica Bretl Milburn, for giving me a run for my money as Chi Omega's Most Humorous Award for the Class of 2008, for bringing light, joy and plenty of edge to my life, for seeing the potential in me, for helping me through every major life crisis.

Boppy Rosenberg White, Michelle Wei, Caitlin Kelly Winter and Kat Pike Herro, for helping me adjust to life as an adult in Minneapolis. To Alyssa Friedlander Levine, Lynn Yeung Huang, and Karena Bibbins McKeever, for being my ride-or-dies in DC. My "peak performance partner" Jenny Westercamp, who pushed me past my upper limit to write this and is one of the very best influences in my life. Her daily texts of encouragement have helped me more than words can say.

Erica Hastings, for being the best crazy plant lady slash motivational speaker to walk this Earth. My Selfie Tuesday ladies, my Sunday Brunch Mastermind ladies, connecting with you every week has been a true delight and each of you has helped me in so many ways you'll never know.

My many teachers, especially Kelly Ditmars who gave me the E.E. Cummings poem and mantra that centered me and helped me stay true to myself in high school, and Pam Kalafut, first my art teacher but then went on to be the biggest influence of my formative years, helping me realize the things that made me unique could be assets, and pushing me to live up to my potential even to this day.

And the motley crew of people hired to put this together, including my editor, Travis May; my graphic designer, Kostis Pavlou; my web designer, Jack Lowrie, and my agent, Tim Grahl. To Vern Cowles, my trainer and friend who pushed me to write this, and his friends at Optimus that recorded it for me. To my Internet spirit animal Lizzy Purcell, for being my beta test reader of this book, and for replying to *literally* every single thing I've created since she first found my work, which has been the biggest creative support I could ever ask for in this world.

To everyone who has supported and helped me along the way, encouraging and growing me into a better version of myself through the gifts of their joy, energy and passion.

SOURCES, BECAUSE THESE IDEAS AREN'T ALL MINE

References

Introduction

The Top 5 Regrets of the Dying, by Bronnie Ware
In Search of Identity, by Anwar Sedat
Perfectly Yourself, by Matthew Kelly
"Basics of Identity," PsychologyToday.com

Chapter 1, Who the eff am I?

A Guide to the Good Life by William B. Irvine
Living Buddha, Living Christ by Thich Nhat Hanh
The Master Key System by Charles Haanel
In Search of Identity by Anwar Al Sadat
Perfectly Yourself by Matthew Kelly
The Divine Dance by Richard Rohr
"How to stop screwing yourself over," TEDx by Mel Robbins
20 Major Philosophers and Their Big Ideas by David A. Tomar

Chapter 2, Why am I running around in this meat suit?

Introduction to Quantum Physics by A.P. French and E.F. Taylor
The Paradox of Choice by Barry Schwartz
The Alchemist by Paulo Coelho
The Defining Decade by Dr. Meg Jay

The Compound Effect by Darren Hardy
Start with Why by Simon Sinek
Called to Create by Jordan Raynor
How Will You Measure Your Life by Clayton Christensen
Bl. John Duns Scotus, FranciscanArchive.org

Chapter 3, Speaking of my meat suit, is there a user guide?

Lean for Life by Louise Parker
Always Hungry by Daniel Ludwig
The Plant Paradox by Dr. Stephen Gundry
How Not to Die by Dr. Michael Greger
The 4-Hour Body by Tim Ferriss
Younger by Harold Lancer
Younger Skin Starts in the Gut by Nigma Talib
We Can Do Better Improving the Health of the American People by Steven A. Schroeder, M.D.
Global Chronic Disease Management Market by Zion Market Research
Health and Economic Costs of Chronic Diseases, CDC.gov

Chapter 4, What about that big blob of cholesterol that tells me what to do?

Essentialism by Greg McKeown
The Servant by James C. Hunter
The Power of Now by Eckhart Tolle
15 Invaluable Laws of Growth by John C. Maxwell
How to Win Friends and Influence People by Dale Carnegie
Awaken the Giant Within by Tony Robbins
Anwar el-Sadat Facts and Biography, NobelPrize.org
The Heart-Brain Connection by The Institute of Heart Math, heartmath.com
The Elegant Universe by Brain Greene
Introducing Eastern Orthodox Theology by Andrew Louth

Giants of Science: Guglielmo Marconi : Radio Pioneer by Beverley Birch

Chapter 5, Who the eff are these people?

Perfectly Yourself by Matthew Kelly
Stumbling on Happiness by Daniel Gilbert
Scary Close by Don Miller
Loneliness is a Killer by David Derbyshire, Daily Mail

Chapter 6, What am I supposed to do about money?

Tap Dancing to Work by Warren Buffet
I Will Teach You to be Rich by Ramit Sethi
The Law of Divine Compensation by Marianne Williamson
You are a Badass at Making Money by Jen Sincero
Use What You've Got by Barbara Corcoran
Think and Grow Rich by Napoleon Hill
How I Conquered My Fear of Going Broke by Farnoosh Torabi, Time Magazine
Scarcity by Sendhil Mullainathan and Eldar Shafir
The History of Money by Rebecca Burn-Callander, The Telegraph
Mindset: The New Psychology of Success by Carol Dweck
Choose Yourself by James Altucher

Chapter 7, When am I supposed to have this all figured out?

Surely You Must be Joking Mr. Feynman by Richard Feynman
The Big Leap by Gay Hendricks
The Subtle Art of Not Giving a F*ck by Mark Manson
Life is What You Make It by Warren Buffet

HI, IT'S ME, THE AUTHOR

About

Colleen Bordeaux is a human capital management consultant, writer and acclaimed speaker on human potential, well-being and the future of work. Her writing has been featured in Huffington Post, Refinery29 and other notable media outlets. She lives in Chicago, IL with her husband Wes and rescue dog Sophie, in a rowhouse they're fixing up themselves because Colleen's obsession with unmet potential also applies to real estate. You can find more of her work at colleenbordeaux.com, including all of the supplemental resources mentioned in this book.